Trailing Down Channel

Bill McDonald

Opus Book Publishing Limited

Trailing Down Channel

A guide for skippers of trailed craft to 260 launching sites on the French coast from Flanders to the Loire and the Western Rivers

by
Bill McDonald

Opus Book Publishing Limited

First Edition 1998

Cover Design: Dave Steele
Cover Illustration & maps: Keith Huggett
Printed in Great Britain by: Biddles Ltd, Guildford, Surrey

Published by
OPUS Book Publishing Ltd
Millhouse, Riseden Road, Wadhurst, East Sussex, TN5 6NY

Copyright: Bill McDonald and Opus Book Publishing Limited 1998

ISBN: 1 898574-08-1

All rights reserved. No part of this publication may be reproduced, stored in a retrieval system, or transmitted in any form or by any means, electronic, mechanical, photocopying, recording or otherwise without the prior permission of the publishers.

Whilst every care has been taken in the compilation of this guide to ensure accuracy, neither the publishers nor the author will hold themselves responsible for errors, omissions or alterations in this publication. They will at all times be grateful to receive information to assist in the updating and accuracy of this publication.

Contents

Introduction ... 7

Emergencies ... 13

1. Flanders, the Pas de Calais and Picardy ... 14

2. Normandy ... 28

3. North Brittany ... 48

4. South Brittany ... 74

5. Western Rivers ... 102

Glossary ... 111

Index ... 115

INTRODUCTION

Considering the number of larger yachts making cross-Channel cruises each year, it is surprising that more skippers and crews of trailed craft do not cruise the French coast the easy way by starting their holiday aboard a ferry or Shuttle.

The aim of this book is to make French cruising for small craft simpler and more attractive by offering a comprehensive directory of launching sites and facilities on the French coast as well as a practical guide to trailer sailing, perhaps for the first time, in a neighbouring country.

By trailing to France, fascinating new cruising grounds become a possibility for small craft of all kinds, sail and power, large and small. Nor are the pleasures of French cruising to be found solely afloat; France's Channel and Atlantic coasts have long been an adventure playground for lovers of fine food and wine, and a fascinating history trail leading us from the earliest European civilisations down to the present day. Come and share it with us!

USING THIS GUIDE

The launching sites are listed in East-West order, beginning on the Belgian frontier and continuing down North-South to the Breton Atlantic coast and the Loire estuary. The seagoing section is followed by a guide to launching sites on the rivers of Brittany and Western France. Each region of France is preceded by a sketch map showing the location of the principal sites, and there is an index at the end of the book. Each site is described, as far as possible, in the following detail:

Type of site: ramp, hard etc.

Suitability: from cruisers down to dinghies and ultralights.

Availability: tidal or other operational limitations.

Restrictions: imposed by tide, regulations, port operations etc.

Shore Facilities: availability of fuel, car and trailer parking, water, toilets, chandlery, boatyards, local shopping facilities, telephones.

Charges: while most launching sites in France remain free for craft not requiring a crane or other assistance, charges are made for launching, especially for larger craft, in some ports. These and a guide to overnight mooring charges, correct for 1998, are given wherever possible, and a contact telephone number, usually of a harbourmaster or sailing club, for those seeking further information, is also supplied.

Definitions: sites are described as being suitable for craft up to the size of Cruisers, Dayboats, Dinghies or Ultralights such as canoes and boards.

Cruisers are craft up to the largest craft capable of being towed by larger family cars, typically around 22ft LOA and some 1.5 tonnes towing weight.

Dayboats assumes craft of up to some 18ft LOA and 500kg or so.

Dinghies includes all small craft capable of being manoeuvred on a trailer or launching trolley by their crew without assistance.

Ultralights will be capable of being carried and launched by their crew without the need for a launching trolley.

BEFORE YOU GO

Remember that although the regulations are much more straightforward than they were a few years ago, trailing to France involves a little more preparation than trailing to another part of the British Isles. Although small boats in Britain do not have to be registered for use in British waters, to go to another EU country you will need a registration document to show that your boat is British-based. One advantage of this is that you will have to comply only with British requirements on such matters as the safety equipment your boat carries: the regulations for French boats in their own waters are both complicated to British eyes and very comprehensively policed. British registration, can be obtained for most craft from the Small Ships Register at the Driver and Vehicle Licensing Agency, Swansea. Showing your registration number, as well as being compulsory, will give considerable peace of mind! It will take some time for Swansea to process your registration, so apply well in advance of your departure date.

Although insurance for small craft in France is not compulsory, it is as sensible to have cover as it is in Britain. If you are already insured, remember to tell your insurer that you are planning to take your boat to France, otherwise your cover may be invalidated. It should also be borne in mind that the French maritime authorities have developed the practice in recent years of charging - usually a substantial sum - for search and rescue operations in the event of a lifeboat or rescue helicopter turnout. While this is almost certainly illegal in international law, such charges will continue to be made until the French government is successfully challenged in the courts at an international level. If you should find yourself faced with such a situation, it is better that an insurer's legal department take up the issue than that you should stand alone against the French government. Make sure, therefore, that your insurance will cover you in such an eventuality.

In recent years, many nasty tales have circulated concerning the need for driving licences for small-boat sailors in France. It should be understood that this does NOT apply to sailing craft. Skippers of British power craft of over 6hp - not sailing craft with auxiliary engines - are however required to be in possession of an appropriate Royal Yachting Association Power Boat

Certificate and/or International Helmsman's Certificate. Details of both these certificates are available from the RYA at RYA House, Romsey Road, Eastleigh, Hampshire SO5 4YA. You can also obtain current information from the RYA as to the safety equipment which is compulsory for your boat - in Britain, this is rather minimal - and the longer list of what is regarded as sensible and is recommended for craft of your size and type.

TRAILING IN FRANCE

Here, once again, the situation is much simpler than it was a few years ago, although there are one or two anomalies which are worth remembering if you need to lend a trailer or ask a French friend to drive for you. Basically the British trailer regulations are now the European regulations. If your trailer is road legal in Britain, it will be road legal in France. If your trailer was professionally built in Britain after 1989, it will certainly conform to the European construction and use regulations. If your trailer is older, or amateur-built, it might be worth referring to the *Trailer Manual* published by Indespension Ltd, and usually available from Indespension stockists, to check on specific requirements. For older trailers these requirements are principally those of structural soundness and that they should fall within the permitted dimensions, which are given in the Manual. It is also a requirement that on braked trailers, the handbrake should be capable of holding the trailer and its load on a gradient of up to 18%. You may feel it worth checking this for yourself before you put it to the test on a steep launching ramp somewhere in Brittany! The trailer lighting regulations have once again been standardised across Europe, so that if your lighting equipment is legal in Britain, and the exact details of this are once again given in the Manual, you will be legal in France.

The principal differences between French and British practice which still exist, and of which you should be aware, concern the registration of larger trailers. While British trailers carry the registration number of their towing vehicle whatever their size, French trailers of over 500kg gross weight have to be registered and insured in their own right. This could be of importance if your boat has to be towed in an emergency by a hired vehicle or breakdown vehicle, when you may have to stress that yours is a British trailer and falls under British regulations in this respect. If your trailer outfit's weight is over 750kg, check that your driving licence covers you for Group E, which includes these larger trailers. Recently issued British licences may not include this group automatically and in future the system will be the same as in France under which Group E has to be specifically applied for and a medical certificate will be required similar to that necessary for British HGV licences. While this will may not be of importance to you, it will be important to a French driver helping out in an emergency.

BEFORE YOU LAUNCH

Seamanlike common sense calls for an informed investigation of waters which are new to you. This guide is not intended as a navigational manual, and it is advisable, especially for skippers of larger craft, to obtain charts and wherever possible a cruising guide to the waters they intend to sail. A set of tide tables as contained in all nautical almanacs are also worth obtaining in advance; alternatively a local tide table can usually be obtained from a chandlery or harbourmaster's office. It is also sensible to investigate any local restrictions such as speed limits or limited zones for different activities such as boardsailing or water skiing which may be in force. Most such restrictions in France are marked by signs ashore or buoys.

There are special navigation rules for personal watercraft in France which were developed following a series of horrendous accidents. They apply to visiting PWCs as well as French craft. The essential provisions are that PWCs must keep to their designated channels where these exist, usually an approach to a beach, and must not navigate by night. PWCs are not permitted more than a mile offshore, and there is a national speed limit of 5 knots within 300 metres of the shore and 3 knots within the confines of any port.

While French sailors in their own waters are limited to staying within statutory distances offshore depending on the type approval rating of their boats and level of safety equipment, these restrictions do not apply to visiting craft, so that you can be guided by seamanlike common sense in this respect. The rule of the road at sea is, of course, International, and the Collision Regulations to which you are accustomed in British waters will apply to you in the same way in France.

CHARTS AND BOOKS

If you are cruising in France for the first time, especially with a cruiser or other larger craft, a set of charts for your intended cruising ground will be essential.

While British chandlers always stock Channel passage charts, it is well worth going to the extra effort of obtaining more detailed charts of the French coast. These may be obtained in Britain either by placing an order with your chandler or direct from the Hydrographic Office, Taunton, Somerset TA1 2 DN, Tel.01823 337900. The catalogue you will need to make your selection is the *Home Waters Catalogue*. If you prefer to obtain French charts, virtually all French chandlers carry a good stock of local charts. The French catalogue, if you wish to order charts, is the *Receuil a l'usage des Plaisanciers*, which is sent free on demand from the French hydrographic service, EPSHOM, BP 426, 29275 Brest Cedex, France.

If your French cruise is your only major voyage of the year, it might be worth buying the French nautical almanac, *"Votre Livre de Bord"*, from a chandler on arrival. Costing FF96 in 1998, it gives a comprehensive set of tide tables, lights and details of ports for larger craft, while the essential parts of the text are repeated in French and English.

Trailer cruising calls for a good road atlas as well as charts, especially if you are seeking out some of the many small and secret sites reached by minor roads, where even in the late 1990s you may be the only boat in the vicinity. Most French drivers regard the Michelin atlas as being by far the best and more accurate in some cases than the official IGN walkers' maps.

Weather forecasts are, if anything, more important in unfamiliar waters than they are on your own coasts. Up-to-date weather bulletins are posted at all French harbourmasters' offices, which often also feature a weather map and barometer. If your French is good, the Meteo France broadcasts can be used to supplement the BBC bulletins, and details of these can once again be found at any harbourmaster's office.

ASHORE IN FRANCE

A long-ago guide book once described the French as "The Most Different" of our near neighbours, and it is a fact that despite the long, slow move towards harmonisation not only of European regulations but of European culture, France retains a refreshingly different and individualistic atmosphere in some respects compared with, say, the Netherlands or Belgium. However, while we may echo the French cry of "Vive La Difference", it can be problematical at times when we are faced with planning a first trailer cruise on unfamiliar ground.

Although tourism is one of France's largest industries, exploring the coast with a small trailed boat is a fairly individual way to spend a holiday. If your boat is not a cruiser and you have to find overnight hotels or campsites for short stays of one or two nights rather than the week or more to which much of the French industry is geared, a certain amount of planning may be necessary, especially if your holiday falls during the peak month of August, when camp sites and hotels are likely to be fully booked on most of the more popular stretches of coast. A little forward planning however can save an awful lot of frustration, and organisations such as the French Tourist Office, Piccadilly, the AA or RAC or some more resourceful travel agents are able to supply contact addresses or brochures for the French regional or departmental (county) tourist offices. All of these will have English speaking staff, and will be able to supply comprehensive details of accommodation in their area as well as a great deal of general information about holiday, cultural and other activities and attractions.

Another possible lead is the *"Logis do France"* brochure, available in many bookshops as well as from tourist offices. These small, independently run hotels and country inns offer a taste of the old, pre-MacDonald's France; a taste in more senses than one, as an evening meal in any of the Logis is everything you would expect of a family run establishment in France. If, of course, you are planning to explore one section of coastline rather than working your way, say, round Brittany, a holiday cottage may be a useful alternative. Apart from the official *"Gites de France"* organisation, which may be contacted through regional tourist offices, the main ferry companies also offer their own holiday cottage brochures, or you may prefer the *"Chez Nous"* organisation which has the advantage of putting you in direct contact with gite owners, the vast majority of whom are English-speaking, at least as a second language.

If your boat is a cruiser, and you are planning to stay overnight in marinas or the yacht basins of the older ports, do remember that visitors' berths are often limited in number, and that these coasts are very popular cruising grounds in summer. A contact telephone number is given for most of the ports offering visitors' berths in this guide, and most harbourmasters or marina managers speak at least some English. Overnight charges in French yachting ports vary as dramatically as they do in Britain, and the rate for a boat of 7m LOA, probably the largest typical trailed cruiser, appears in the guide in most cases.

Because many French cruiser skippers prefer to sail from marina to marina, it is still possible, in Brittany especially, to find quiet overnight anchorages in creeks and inlets, especially if your boat, like most trailed craft, will take the ground comfortably. This is particularly so if your cruise falls outside the school holiday period, when you could easily find yourself sailing an estuary or bay with only a few local boats for company, or, come to that, not so much as another boat under way: an experience not to be missed, taking us back as it does to cruising as it was known to an earlier generation of leisure sailors.

EMERGENCIES

While rescue and medical services in France are very similar to their British counterparts, the means of alerting them and the way in which they are organised are radically different. The information which follows may therefore be instrumental in saving someone's life and we recommend that you photocopy this page and keep a copy available in your car or boat.

VHF Mayday and PanPan transmissions.

The radio procedure for emergencies is international, and an English language transmission will certainly be understood by French coastguards and almost certainly by most other maritime professionals. If, therefore, you have VHF, proceed as you would in British waters. French coastguards maintain a 24 hour listening watch on Channel 16, and plan to continue to do so when the new international procedure is introduced in February 1999.

Injury - Obtaining an ambulance.

The enmergency ambulance service in France is operated by the fire service, Les Sapeurs-Pompiers. They are contacted by **dialling 18**. Like British 999 calls, these calls are free. Remember that the operator may not speak English. If this is the case, stress that you need an AMBULANCE - the word is the same - and that someone is injured - BLESSE - and give the location of the telephone from which you are calling.

Paramedics

In the case of serious injury, drowning, cardiac arrest etc., immediately after calling the Pompiers, call the paramedic service (SAMU) by **dialling 15** - again a free call. Give them the same information; the key words here are probably :- Drowning - NOYADE; Asphyxiation - the same word in both languages: and Heart attack - INFARCTUS. The pompiers will probably arrive first, and will do their best to resuscitate the casualty while waiting for the SAMU paramedics with their specialist training and equipment.

Incident at sea - Search and rescue.

THERE IS NO NATIONAL EMERGENCY NUMBER TO ALERT THE COASTGUARD OR LIFEBOAT. Phone the nearest of the search and rescue co-ordination centres (CROSS in French) listed below. If you get the wrong one, they will relay the information for you. The operator will speak English.

1. Gris Nez. Tel: 03 21 87 21 87 - from the Belgian Frontier to Cap d'Antifer, Normandy.
2. Jobourg Tel: 02 33 52 72 13 - Cap d'Antifer to Mont St Michel
3. Corsen Tel: 02 98 89 31 31 - Mont St Michel to Penmarch, Brittany
4. Etel Tel: 02 97 55 35 35 - The whole Atlantic coast South of Penmarch

THESE ARE NOT FREE CALLS. If you have no phone card or change for the few remaining coin operated boxes, call the Fire Brigade on 17 or the police on 18 and ask them to relay your call.

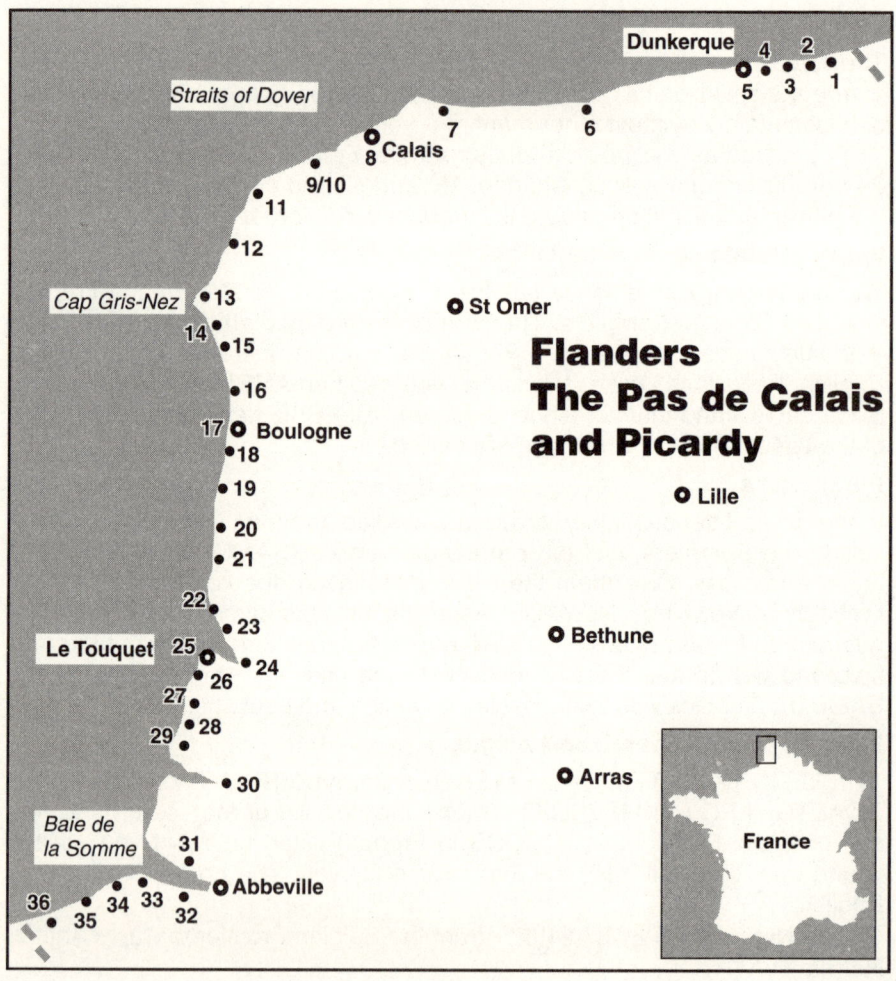

1. Bray-Dunes

Type:	ramp to soft sand beach
Suits:	dinghies
Availability:	all states of the tide but best towards HW as sands uncover for several hundred metres
Restrictions:	national inshore speed limit
Facilities:	shopping, telephones in town centre: first aid post and toilets on promenade: inshore lifeboat: parking for cars and trailers, may be crowded in summer: sand yacht hire
Charge:	none
Directions:	from A16 (E40) or N1, via D947 following signs for Bray-Dunes to town centre: best ramp is at east end of promenade: poorer ramp exists at western end
Waters accessed:	North Sea

2. Zuydcoote

Type:	ramp to soft beach
Suits:	dinghies
Availability:	all states of the tide but best towards HW as sands uncover for several hundred metres
Restrictions:	national inshore speed limit
Facilities:	parking for cars and trailers, may be crowded in summer: cafes, basic shopping and telephones in town centre: camp sites nearby
Charge:	none
Directions:	from A16 or N1, follow signs for Zuydcoote and continue through town centre to beach car park: ramp is at seaward side
Waters accessed:	North Sea

3. Leffrinckoucke

Type:	whole of promenade forms ramp to beach
Suits:	dinghies
Availability:	all states of the tide but best towards HW as sands uncover for several hundred metres
Restrictions:	national inshore speed limit
Facilities:	parking for car and trailer: first aid post, inshore lifeboat and toilets grouped in prominent position: basic shopping, cafes and telephones in town centre
Charge:	none
Directions:	from A16 or N1, follow signs for Leffrinckoucke and proceed through town centre to seafront
Waters accessed:	North Sea

4. Malo-les-Bains

Type:	ramp to beach at east end of promenade
Suits:	dinghies
Availability:	all states of the tide but best towards HW as sands uncover for several hundred metres
Restrictions:	national inshore speed limit
Facilities:	parking for car and trailer, may be crowded in summer: shopping and telephones in town centre
Charge:	none
Directions:	from A16 and N1 via D4, following signs for Malo-les-Bains. **Take care** - extremely dangerous "priorite a droite" system in town centre: proceed through town centre to seafront
Waters accessed:	North Sea

5. Dunkirk / Dunkerque
Tel: 03 28 29 72 61 (Harbour Master)
03 28 66 79 90 (Yacht Club de la Mer du Nord)

Type:	slips at yacht club and Quai de Leughenaer (fishermen's slip) in tidal port
Suits:	cruisers
Availability:	within 3 hrs HW: fishermen's slip may be obstructed and workboats have priority
Restrictions:	speed limits apply in port: sailing craft must proceed under power in harbour: water sports prohibited
Facilities:	parking for car and trailer: pontoon berths for cruisers: toilets, showers: water & electricity on pontoons: telephones: fuel from yacht club: crane: overnight berth 7m, FF70: shopping in town centre: offshore lifeboat station
Charge:	yes, for larger craft and powerboats
Directions:	from A16 or N1, follow signs for Dunkerque and proceed to town centre, Port du Grand Large and Capitainerie
Waters accessed:	North Sea and French inland waterway system

6. Gravelines / Petit and Grand Fort Philippe
Tel: 03 28 23 19 45 (Harbour Master) 03 28 65 21 28 (Tourist Office)

Type:	(1) Petit Fort Philippe slip on east side of outer port near sailing club, (2) Grand Fort Philippe ramp to soft sand on west side of outer port near lifeboat station
Suits:	cruisers
Availability:	cruisers best to launch towards HW, smaller craft at all states of tide: east site best below half ebb
Restrictions:	speed limit applies in harbour
Facilities:	in outer port: toilets, water point by visitors' pontoons, parking for car and trailer: shopping, and telephones in town centre: fuel from local garages: lifeboat station: chandler: boatyard,

	repairs to timber, GRP, engineering: overnight berth in inner basin, for 7m, FF42
Charge:	none for launching or outer harbour
Directions:	from A16 or N1, via D218 following signs for Gravelines and Petit Fort Philippe (east side) or Grand Fort Philippe (west side)
Waters accessed:	North Sea and French inland waterway system

7. Les Hemmes

Type:	sandy access gap to soft beach
Suits:	dinghies
Availability:	possible at any state of tide but best towards HW
Restrictions:	national inshore speed limit
Facilities:	limited parking for car and trailer
Charge:	none
Directions:	from coastal D119 between Gravelines and Calais, follow signs for Les Hemmes and then for Les Palominos (not a riding stables but a camp site) down minor country road
Waters accessed:	North Sea

8. Calais
Tel: 03 21 96 31 20 (Harbour Master) 03 21 34 55 23 (Yacht Harbour)

Type:	broad stone ramp to hard sand
Suits:	cruisers
Availability:	cruisers best towards HW: smaller craft at all times
Restrictions:	outside harbour, national inshore speed limit: inside harbour, special traffic restrictions apply: obtain local information from harbour master if intending to navigate inside port. **Caution:** this is an extremely busy ferry port
Facilities:	parking for cars and trailers near ramp: shopping of all kinds in town and at nearby hypermarkets: fuel from hypermarkets and garages: full yacht harbour facilities exist for larger craft in inner port: overnight berth for 7m, from FF21
Charge:	none for launching outside harbour
Directions:	from Calais town centre, follow signs for La Plage and continue to local youth leisure centre: ramp is nearby, just outside harbour mole
Waters accessed:	North Sea, Channel and French inland waterway system

9. Sangatte

Type:	gap in dunes to soft beach
Suits:	dinghies
Availability:	all states of tide but best towards HW
Restrictions:	national inshore speed limit
Facilities:	parking for cars and trailers may be crowded in summer
Charge:	none

Directions:	from Calais follow coastal D940 to northern outskirts of Sangatte
Waters accessed:	North Sea and Channel

10. Sangatte South

Type:	concrete ramp to soft beach
Suits:	dinghies
Availability:	all states of tide but best towards HW
Restrictions:	ramp must be kept clear for lifeboat: parking on ramp or approach forbidden: national inshore speed limit
Facilities:	parking for cars and trailers nearby limited, may be crowded in summer: shopping and telephones in Sangatte village: inshore lifeboat
Charge:	none
Directions:	follow coastal D940 to southern end of Sangatte and take minor road to sea
Waters accessed:	North Sea and Channel

11. Cap Blanc Nez

Type:	steep path to beach
Suits:	ultralights
Availability:	all states of tide
Restrictions:	none
Facilities:	limited parking for cars on minor road
Charge:	none
Directions:	from Calais follow coastal D940 to just south of Blanc Nez: at foot of a steep hill is a small unmarked access road leading to a restricted-width barrier; launching trolleys can pass this, but the path beyond is steep and shoud be attempted only with portageable craft
Waters accessed:	North Sea and Channel

12. Wissant

Type:	concrete ramp to soft beach
Suits:	dinghies
Availability:	all states of tide
Restrictions:	national inshore speed limit: activity zones may be in place in summer
Facilities:	basic shopping, garage, telephones etc. in village: rescue station on beach in summer: limited parking nearby
Charge:	none
Directions:	follow coastal D940 to Wissant village and enter village centre: access to beach via minor roads is unmarked and is to the south of village centre: ramp is to be found at north end of the sea front, near CRS rescue station
Waters accessed:	Channel

13. Cap Gris Nez

Type:	steep ramp to stone and sand beach
Suits:	dinghies
Availability:	all states of tide but recovery best towards HW
Restrictions:	national inshore speed limit
Facilities:	parking for cars and trailers: telephone in village: nearby cafe
Charge:	none
Directions:	follow D940, then D191 south of Audinghem to Cap Gris Nez, follow signs for La Plage: ramp is near Hotel la Sirene
Waters accessed:	Channel

14. Audresselles

Type:	gaps to hard sand beach to north and south of village
Suits:	dinghies
Availability:	all states of tide
Restrictions:	national inshore speed limit: fishermen have priority
Facilities:	limited parking for car and trailer nearby: basic shopping and telephone in village: garage nearby on coast road
Charge:	none
Directions:	follow D940 to village: first gap is on seaward side at north end of village: other roads to sea in village are marked 'No Entry', but tend to be used by local fishermen: second gap is to be found at south end of village and is also visible from coast road
Waters accessed:	Channel

15. Ambleteuse

Type:	stone ramp to hard sand and stone beach
Suits:	dinghies
Availability:	best above half-tide on account of rocks uncovered below this point
Restrictions:	national inshore speed limit
Facilities:	basic shopping and telephone in village: parking for car and trailer
Charge:	none
Directions:	from D940, follow signs for Ambleteuse village centre, then for La Plage
Waters accessed:	Channel

16. Wimereux

Type:	paths from town centre to beach
Suits:	ultralights
Availability:	all states of tide
Restrictions:	activity zones may be in force in summer

Facilities:	shopping and telephones in town centre: parking for cars not trailers, may be crowded in summer: toilets on sea front
Charge:	none
Directions:	Wimereux is on D940: parking areas for beach are towards north end of town: follow stream flowing through town to beach
Waters accessed:	Channel

17. Boulogne
Tel: 03 21 99 62 00 (Harbour Master) 03 21 31 70 01 (Yacht Harbour)

Type:	ramp to hard sand beach: slipway at yacht harbour in inner port
Suits:	ramp: dinghies; yacht harbour: cruisers
Availability:	ramp best towards HW as tide ebbs several hundred metres
Restrictions:	activity zones in force within harbour area: speed limits apply: traffic restrictions: information from Harbour Master or yacht harbour
Facilities:	parking may be difficult in summer, especially for trailers: nearby sailing club parking area may be used - ask permission when anyone present: shopping, telephones etc. in town centre: yacht harbour has showers, toilets, water and electricity to pontoons, fuel, crane: overnight berth for 7m boat, FF77
Charge:	for ramp, none
Directions:	ramp is just north of the town on entering via coast road (D940): sailing club ramp towards south end of same beach: yacht harbour - follow signs for ferry terminal
Waters accessed:	Channel

18. Le Portel

Type:	ramp to soft sand beach
Suits:	dinghies
Availability:	all states of tide but best towards HW
Restrictions:	national inshore speed limit: hovercraft zone to north of beach is a prohibited area
Facilities:	parking for cars and trailers: water; toilets; telephones etc. in Le Portel centre
Charge:	none
Directions:	from Boulogne take coastal D119: Le Portel is the southern suburb of Boulogne: in Le Portel, follow signs - difficult to spot - for La Plage
Waters accessed:	Channel

19. Equihen Plage

Type:	ramp to sandy beach
Suits:	dinghies
Availability:	all states of tide but best within 3hrs HW
Restrictions:	national inshore speed limit
Facilities:	parking for cars and trailers, telephone, toilets: first aid post in summer: basic shopping in village
Charge:	none
Directions:	from Boulogne follow coastal D119: at Equihen, follow signs for La Plage
Waters accessed:	Channel

20. Hardelot Plage

Type:	ramp to soft sand beach
Suits:	dinghies
Availability:	all states of tide but best within 3hrs HW
Restrictions:	national inshore speed limit: activity zones in force in summer
Facilities:	parking for cars and trailers, may be crowded in summer: toilets, telephones, basic shopping in town
Charge:	none at public ramp
Directions:	from N1 and D940 take D113E, following signs for Hardelot Plage: signs for Base Nautique lead to sailing club: public launching ramp is at north end of beach
Waters accessed:	Channel

21. Dunes de Mont St Frieux

Type:	wooden ramp to hard sand beach
Suits:	dinghies; dayboats if towing vehicle is 4x4
Availability:	all states of tide but best within 3hrs HW
Restrictions:	national inshore speed limit
Facilities:	limited wild parking for car and trailer
Charge:	none
Directions:	from coastal D940, follow signs for Dunes de Mont St Frieux
Waters accessed:	Channel

22. Ste Cecilie Plage

Type:	ramp to hard sand beach
Suits:	dinghies
Availability:	all states of tide but best within 3hrs HW
Restrictions:	national inshore speed limit: activity zones may be in force in summer
Facilities:	parking for car and trailer; toilets; first aid post; shopping, telephones etc. in town centre
Charge:	none

Directions:	from coastal D940, follow signs for Ste Cecilie Plage, then La Plage
Waters accessed:	Channel

23. St Gabriel Plage

Type:	sandy ramp to hard beach
Suits:	dinghies
Availability:	all states of tide but best within 3hrs HW
Restrictions:	national inshore speed limit
Facilities:	limited wild parking for cars and trailers: camp site nearby
Charge:	none
Directions:	from D940, follow signs for St Gabriel Plage: badly surfaced road leads to sandy track to beach, suitable for light trailers or launching trolleys
Waters accessed:	Channel

24. Etaples
Tel: 03 21 84 54 33 (Harbour Master) 03 21 94 74 26 (Centre Nautique)

Type:	hard ramp to creek: also yacht harbour
Suits:	cruisers towards HW, small craft 2hrs either side HW
Availability:	ramp best towards HW as tide ebbs several hundred metres
Restrictions:	national inshore speed limit
Facilities:	parking for cars and trailers at Centre Nautique: chandlery on site, others in town: fuel from local garages: toilets and water at Centre Nautique or yacht harbour: boatyards offering repairs etc.: shopping in town centre: overnight anchorage in estuary free for cruisers, overnight berth in yacht harbour for 7m, FF60
Charge:	none for launching at Centre Nautique, who wish to encourage visitors with small boats: ask permission if anyone present in office
Directions:	on entering town via D940, Centre Nautique de la Canche is on right at entrance to town
Waters accessed:	La Canche Estuary and Channel

25. Le Touquet

Type:	sandy ramp to beach outside town: also slipway at yacht club
Suits:	ramp: dinghies: yacht club: cruisers
Availability:	towards HW
Restrictions:	national inshore speed limit: activity zones in force off Le Touquet town beach
Facilities:	shopping, telephones etc. in town centre: toilets, water, electricity and telephones at yacht club: parking free in front of yacht club, paying on coast road
Charge:	none to launch from ramp: charge levied for yacht club facilities
Directions:	from D940 and N39, follow signs for Le Touquet - Paris Plage: to the north of the town beach, a small coast road leads

	through dunes to yacht club: off this road are several sandy gaps where light dinghies may be launched over the beach, although cars and trailers must proceed a few hundred metres more to the parking area by the yacht club
Waters accessed:	La Canche Estuary and Channel

26. Paris Plage

Type:	ramp to hard sand beach
Suits:	dinghies
Availability:	towards HW
Restrictions:	national inshore speed limit: activity zones in force
Facilities:	parking (charge) for cars and trailers, toilets; telephones, rescue station in summer: shopping in town centre
Charge:	yes
Directions:	as for Le Touquet, then follow signs for Paris Plage: the Base Nautique is at the south end of the promenade
Waters accessed:	La Canche Estuary and Channel

27. Stella Plage

Type:	ramp to soft beach
Suits:	dinghies
Availability:	towards HW
Restrictions:	national inshore speed limit: activity zones may be in force in summer
Facilities:	parking for cars and trailers, toilets; telephone, basic shopping in town centre
Charge:	none
Directions:	from D940, take D144, following signs for Stella Plage, then for La Plage: ramp is at north end of beach by large parking area
Waters accessed:	Channel

28. Merlimont Plage

Type:	ramp to soft beach
Suits:	dinghies
Availability:	towards HW
Restrictions:	national inshore speed limit: activity zones may be in force in summer
Facilities:	parking for cars and trailers: toilets, telephone, basic shopping in town centre
Charge:	none
Directions:	from D940, follow D144E, to Merlimont Plage, then signs for La Plage; ramp is at north end of sea front
Waters accessed:	Channel

29. Berck Plage

Type:	concret ramp to beach
Suits:	dayboats
Availability:	2hrs either side HW
Restrictions:	national inshore speed limit
Facilities:	parking for car and trailer, toilets, lifeboat station, telephone, water: shopping etc. in town centre: fuel from nearby garages
Charge:	may be levied for larger boats when anyone present
Directions:	follow D940 to Berck-sur Mer. From town centre, take minor roads towards lighthouse at south end of town and follow signs for Base Nautique
Waters accessed:	Baie de l'Authie and Channel

30. Groffliers

Type:	earth and stone ramp to creek
Suits:	cruisers
Availability:	2hrs either side HW
Restrictions:	national inshore speed limit
Facilities:	basic parking for car and trailer: telephone in nearby cafe
Charge:	none
Directions:	from D940 south of Berck-sur Mer, follow signs for Baie de l'Authie via minor roads as far as Auberge de la Madelon: staithe and ramp opposite
Waters accessed:	Authie Estuary and Channel

31. Le Crotoy
Tel: 03 22 27 80 24 (Mairie)

Type:	(1) ramps to hard beach (2) slip in inner port
Suits:	(1) dinghies (2) cruisers
Availability:	(1) 2hrs either side HW (2) towards HW
Restrictions:	national inshore speed limit: speed limit within port
Facilities:	parking for cars and trailers: fuel from nearby garages; toilets on quay; basic shopping and telephones in town centre, chandlery, boatyard: water and electricity in yacht basin: overnight berth in yacht basin for 7m, FF60
Charge:	none for launching
Directions:	from D940 follow signs to town centre: first ramps to beach are on seaward side of road entering town: yacht basin is at south end of town, approached via fish quay. UNDER NO CIRCUMSTANCES attempt to launch from the training wall at rear of yacht basin, which resembles a slip at some states of tide.
Waters accessed:	Baie de la Somme and Channel

32. St Valery-sur-Somme
Tel: 03 22 60 24 80 (Harbour Master)

Type:	narrow ramps to inner port
Suits:	cruisers
Availability:	cruisers towards HW, small craft 3hrs either side HW
Restrictions:	speed limit in port
Facilities:	parking for cars and trailers: fuel from nearby garage; telephone on quay; toilets and showers in yachting port, shopping etc. in town centre, chandlery, boatyard: overnight berth alongside for 7m, FF62
Charge:	none for launching
Directions:	follow D940, take D3 at roundabout after crossing Canal de la Somme: slip is near canal lock gates, on left bank on seaward side
Waters accessed:	Baie de la Somme, Channel and inland waterways via Somme

33. Cap Hornu

Type:	broad hard at mouth of the Somme Estuary
Suits:	cruisers
Availability:	cruisers towards HW, small craft 3hrs either side HW
Restrictions:	national inshore speed limit
Facilities:	parking for cars and trailers: NOTE: PARK ON HIGH GROUND as much of this area covers at HW springs: telephone nearby
Charge:	none
Directions:	from St Valery, follow D3 signed for Cap Hornu
Waters accessed:	Baie de la Somme and Channel

34. Le Hourdel

Type:	shingle hard
Suits:	cruisers
Availability:	cruisers towards HW, small craft 3hrs either side HW
Restrictions:	national inshore speed limit
Facilities:	parking for cars and trailers: NOTE: PARK ON HIGH GROUND; hard covers at HW springs
Charge:	none
Directions:	from St Valery, via D940 and D3 turn right onto D102, following signs for Le Hourdel: hard is beyond lighthouse
Waters accessed:	Baie de la Somme and Channel

35. Cayeux

Type:	beach launching over shingle bank
Suits:	dinghies
Availability:	all states of tide except dead LW

Restrictions:	national inshore speed limit
Facilities:	parking for cars and trailers: basic shopping, telephones in town centre
Charge:	none
Directions:	follow coastal D3 to sea front: launching is easiest at south end of town
Waters accessed:	Baie de la Somme and Channel

36. Ault

Type:	concrete ramp to hard beach
Suits:	dinghies
Availability:	all states of tide
Restrictions:	national inshore speed limit: activity zones may be in force in summer
Facilities:	parking for cars and trailers, water, and toilets when Base Nautique open; basic shopping, telephones in town
Charge:	none in 1997: permission may be needed from Base Nautique when anyone present
Directions:	from D940, take D463 to Ault; Base Nautique is approached from sea front road
Waters accessed:	Channel

Over 650 coastal slipways in the UK are listed in:

WHERE TO LAUNCH AROUND THE COAST

edited by Diana van der Klugt
ISBN 1-898574 02 0

This popular and useful guide listing over 650 coastal and lake launching sites (inc. Norfolk Broads) for boats up to 25' LOA (approx). A clear format gives the name and location of each site, and where possible a contact phone number. Information, including type of slipway, access, times available, tidal and any other restrictions, speed limits etc, guide to charges, dues and licences required, car parking, local facilities and road directions, follows. The book is arranged in seven geographical areas and has a comprehensive index.

£6.95
+£1 p&p

Introducing the popular world of sailing dinghies

DINGHY & DAYBOAT DIRECTORY

edited by Diana van der Klugt
ISBN 1-898574-04-9

A comprehensive and fully illustrated guide to over 180 different sailing dinghies, dayboats, keelboats and multihulls. Each main entry is headed by a colour photograph of the boat and an illustration of the sail insignia and gives design specifications, a brief history and description of the class, name of designer and builder, number built and name of class secretary. An 'At-a-Glance' index to sail insignia at the front of the book helps easy identification of craft

£7.95
+£1 p&p

available from: Bookshops and Yacht Chandlers or the Publishers,
OPUS Book Publishing Limited
20 East Road, West Mersea, Colchester, Essex.CO5 8EB
Tel / Fax: 01206 383629 e-mail: opus@dmac.co.uk
Credit cards accepted

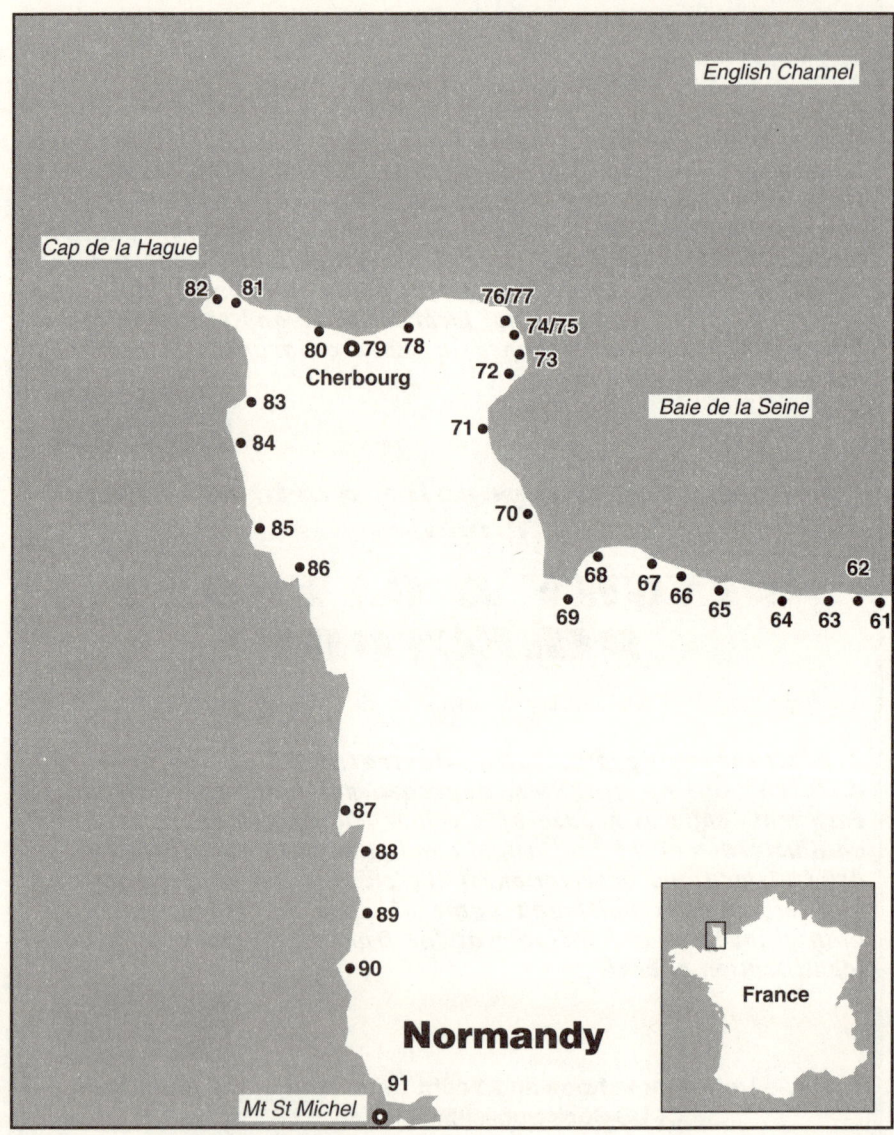

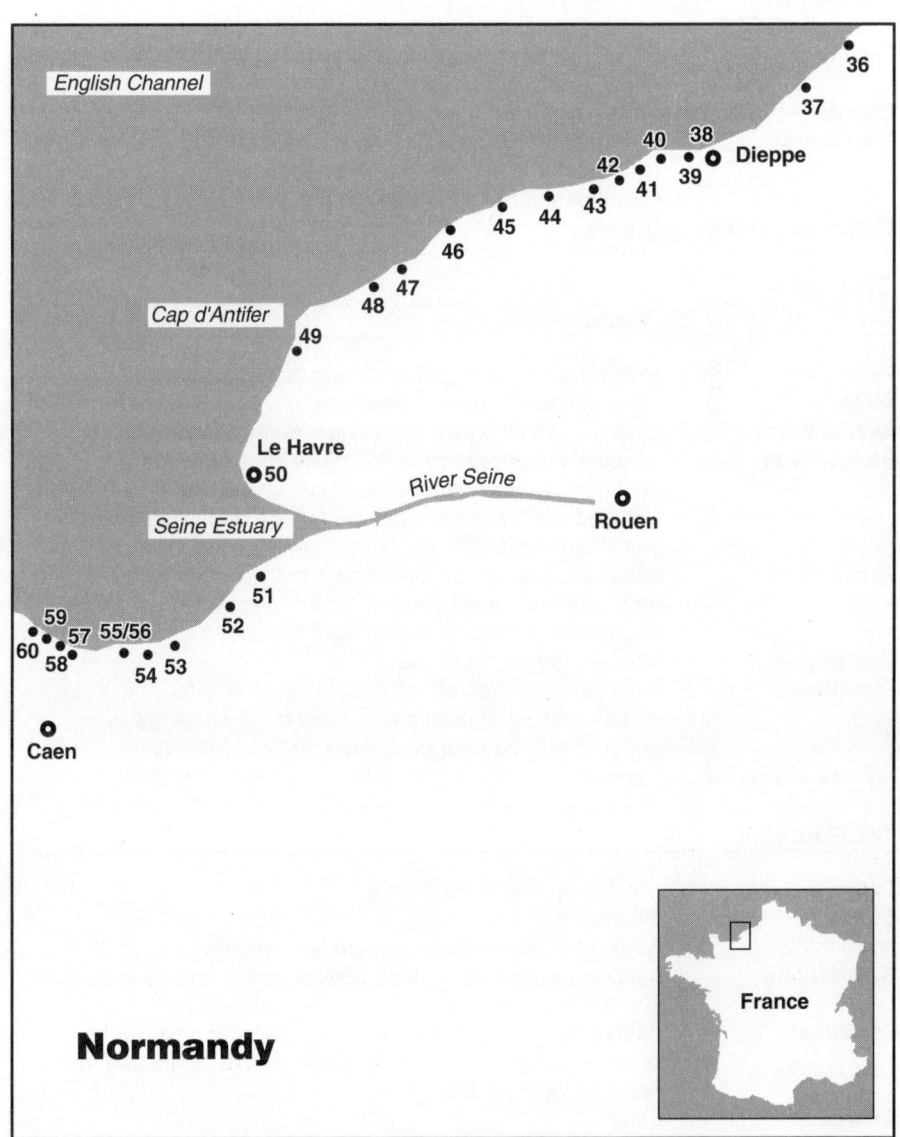

37. Mesnil-Val

Type:	shingle beach launching
Suits:	dinghies
Availability:	within 3hrs HW
Restrictions:	national inshore speed limit:
Facilities:	parking for cars and trailers, may be crowded in summer: telephone in restaurant nearby
Charge:	none
Directions:	from D940 to south of Le Treport, take D126 and follow signs for Mesnil-Val: a gap in the cliffs leads down to a shingle beach near a restaurant
Waters accessed:	Channel

38. Dieppe
Tel: 02 35 40 19 79 (Yacht Harbour)

Type:	launching over shingle beach and in yacht harbour
Suits:	(1) dinghies (2) cruisers (with crane)
Availability:	dinghies, within 3hrs HW: cruisers during working hours
Restrictions:	national inshore speed limit: activity zones may be in force in summer: cruiser skippers note that Dieppe is a busy fishing port and the Transmanche terminal is a prohibited area to pleasure craft; traffic regulations apply in port
Facilities:	beach launching: parking for cars and trailers, may be crowded in summer: yacht harbour: water, electricity, fuel, toilets, showers and chandlery: overnight berth for 7m, FF75
Charge:	none for beach launching
Directions:	least crowded area of sea front in summer is to west of promenade: partly pedestrianised : crew must wheel trolley to beach. Yacht harbour is situated on Quai Henri IV
Waters accessed:	Channel

39. Pourville

Type:	good ramp to shingle landing
Suits:	dinghies
Availability:	within 3hrs HW: local fishermen have priority
Restrictions:	national inshore speed limit: activity zones may be in force in summer
Facilities:	parking for cars and trailers 200m, winching posts for heavier boats on ramp, first aid post, telephones at centre sea front, basic shopping in town
Charge:	none
Directions:	from Dieppe, follow coastal D75 and signs for Pourville: launching ramp is at west of sea front
Waters accessed:	Channel

40. Port l'Ailly

Type:	beach landing
Suits:	dinghies
Availability:	within 3hrs HW
Restrictions:	national inshore speed limit:
Facilities:	basic parking for cars and trailers
Charge:	none
Directions:	take D925 from Dieppe, to D55 following signs first for Varangeville, then for Port l'Ailly: a steep minor road descends through gap in cliffs to a peaceful and secret landing
Waters accessed:	Channel

41. Ste Marguerite / Quiberville

Type:	ramp to shingle beach landing
Suits:	dinghies
Availability:	all states of tide except dead LW
Restrictions:	national inshore speed limit: local fishermen have priority
Facilities:	parking for cars and trailers, toilets, inshore lifeboat
Charge:	none: obtain permission to use better of two ramps from angling club when anyone present
Directions:	this village is on coastal D75: first landing at Ste Marguerite angling club: if ramp blocked by boats, second shingle landing exists to west of Quiberville promenade
Waters accessed:	Channel

42. St Aubin-sur-Mer

Type:	concrete ramp to beach
Suits:	dinghies
Availability:	all states of tide except dead LW
Restrictions:	national inshore speed limit: local fishermen have priority
Facilities:	car park (charge in summer), toilets, telephones and information office
Charge:	none for launching
Directions:	St Aubin is on the coastal D75: in village follow main village street down to sea
Waters accessed:	Channel

43. Veules-les-Roses

Type:	ramp to beach
Suits:	dinghies
Availability:	all states of tide except dead LW
Restrictions:	national inshore speed limit: local fishermen have priority
Facilities:	parking for cars and trailers, may be crowded in summer, toilets, telephones

Charge: none
Directions: from D925 Dieppe - St Valery, take minor road into village centre and downhill to beach
Waters accessed: Channel

44. St Valery-en-Caux
Tel: 02 35 97 01 30 (Harbour Master)

Type: steep ramp into outer harbour
Suits: cruisers
Availability: cruisers towards HW: dinghies within 2hrs HW
Restrictions: speed limit applies in port
Facilities: parking for cars and trailers, lifeboat station, telephones, shopping in town: in yacht harbour, toilets, showers, chandler, cranes and fuel: overnight berth 7m, FF80
Charge: none for launching
Directions: ramp is on inner side of east pier, near lifeboat station: **note** that it is steep and cruisers are best launched by winch from 4x4 vehicle
Waters accessed: Channel

45. Petites Dalles, Grandes Dalles

Type: ramps to beach
Suits: dinghies: dayboats at Grandes Dalles
Availability: within 3hrs HW
Restrictions: national inshore speed limit
Facilities: parking for cars and trailers, toilets, telephone, inshore lifeboat at Petites Dalles
Charge: none
Directions: these are twin villages perched in adjacent clefts in the cliffs, reached in both cases from the coastal D925 and then D5 (for Les Grandes Dalles,take D79 at Sassetot le Mauconduit: then minor roads): local signposting is poor but good map reading helps! In both cases a minor road descends to the sea and a concrete ramp to the beach
Waters accessed: Channel

46. St Pierre-en-Port

Type: concrete ramp to sea in cove
Suits: dayboats
Availability: dayboats within 2hrs HW: dinghies at all states of tide
Restrictions: national inshore speed limit
Facilities: limited parking for cars and trailers
Charge: none
Directions: from the D925, via D33 following signs for St Pierre-en-Port: minor road signed for La Plage leads down to cove
Waters accessed: Channel

47. Fecamp
Tel: 02 35 28 13 58 (Harbour Master)

Type:	slip into outer harbour: also crane
Suits:	dayboats up to 500kg, cruisers by crane
Availability:	within 5hrs HW
Restrictions:	speed limit applies in port
Facilities:	parking for cars and trailers (charge), telephones, toilets, showers, water, electricity on pontoons, diesel from quay, shopping in town centre, chandler, boatyard, overnight berth 7m, FF84
Charge:	yes to launch boats up to 500kg from slip FF20: to park FF10 per day
Directions:	all facilities on west side of harbour: enquiries to reception on outer Quai Vauban
Waters accessed:	Channel

48. Yport

Type:	shingle beach landing
Suits:	dinghies
Availability:	all states of tide
Restrictions:	national inshore speed limit: local fishermen have priority
Facilities:	parking for cars and trailers, may be crowded in summer, toilets, basic shopping, inshore lifeboat
Charge:	none
Directions:	from Fecamp take D940 then D211 following signs for Yport: road descends through village to sea front
Waters accessed:	Channel

49. Havre-Antifer, Port Petrolier

Type:	concrete ramp to shingle beach
Suits:	cruisers
Availability:	cruisers at HW, small craft at all states of tide
Restrictions:	national inshore speed limit: approach channel of main port to be kept clear: no fires or camping ashore
Facilities:	parking for cars and trailers
Charge:	none
Directions:	from D940 take D111E to Plage de Bruneval: shingle cove with ramp lies inside breakwater of tanker port on what is in every other respect a wild and unspoilt coast
Waters accessed:	Channel

50. Le Havre
Tel: 02 35 21 23 95 (Yacht Harbour Master)

Type:	(1) yacht harbour not geared to craft smaller than cruisers: (2) ramp to hard sand beach
Suits:	(1) cruisers, (2) dinghies
Availability:	cruisers during working hours: dinghies within 2hrs HW
Restrictions:	speed limit applies in port: Le Havre port and approaches are intensely busy: traffic regulations apply: enquiries to Harbour Master
Facilities:	parking for cars and trailers, water, electricity on pontoons, toilets, showers, telephones, cranes, chandlers, boatyard, fuel from nearby garages, overnight berth for 7m, FF67
Charge:	yes for cruisers: none for dinghies
Directions:	yacht harbour is to the west of the commercial port: from ferry terminal, proceed as if taking D940 north out of town, then take quayside road down to yacht harbour: dinghy slip faces seawards from main car park
Waters accessed:	Seine Estuary, River Seine and Channel

51. Trouville / Deauville
Tel: 02 31 98 50 40 (Harbour Master)

Type:	broad ramp to outer harbour
Suits:	cruisers
Availability:	cruisers towards HW: small craft within 2 hrs HW: beware of sill 3m below HWM on ramp
Restrictions:	speed limit applies in port
Facilities:	parking for cars and trailers near ramp, may be crowded in summer: shopping in town centre, fuel from local garages: yacht harbour facilities include toilets, showers, telephones: chandlers and boatyards may be found in rear areas of tidal fishing port of Deauville. In yacht harbour overnight berth for 7m, FF68
Charge:	none for launching in tidal outer port
Directions:	in Deauville centre, follow signs for Port Deauville as far as tidal harbour: slip is reached from coach park, and is near harbour master's office
Waters accessed:	Channel and Seine Estuary

52. Blonville

Type:	ramps to hard sand beach
Suits:	dinghies
Availability:	all states of tide but best within 3hrs HW
Restrictions:	national inshore speed limit
Facilities:	parking for cars and trailers
Charge:	none

Directions:	Blonville is on coastal D513: entering from the east a series of sandy ramps give access to beach; the best of these is the westernmost
Waters accessed:	Seine Estuary and Channel

53. Dives-sur-Mer
Tel: 02 31 24 48 00 (Marina Harbour Master)

Type:	concrete ramps to tidal creek leading to inner port
Suits:	cruisers
Availability:	cruisers towards HW: small craft as soon as tide enters creek
Restrictions:	speed limit applies in port: national inshore speed limit outside; activity zones may be in force nearby in summer
Facilities:	parking for cars and trailers, water, telephone, inshore lifeboat in outer port near ramps: inner yacht harbour (Port Guillaume), offers pontoons, showers, toilets, electricity, fuel etc: overnight berth for 7m, FF71
Charge:	none for launching in outer port
Directions:	Dives is on the coastal D513: on entering town, follow sign on right for Le Port, which leads to a concrete ramp just above the fish market: the fishermen's ramp is better but is often obstructed
Waters accessed:	Caen Bay

54. Cabourg

Type:	ramp to hard sand
Suits:	dinghies
Availability:	as soon as tide covers outer flats
Restrictions:	national inshore speed limit
Facilities:	parking for cars and trailers
Charge:	none
Directions:	Cabourg lies to west of Dives Estuary and is reached via D513 and D514: site is not easy to find; follow west side of estuary seawards until ramp appears on right
Waters accessed:	Dives Estuary and Caen Bay

55. Merville

Type:	ramps to hard beach
Suits:	dinghies
Availability:	within 3hrs HW approx.
Restrictions:	national inshore speed limit
Facilities:	parking for cars and trailers, telephone, toilets, lifeguard station
Charge:	none
Directions:	at entrance to Merville, take road to beach: ramp leads from car park to hard sand
Waters accessed:	Caen Bay

56. Franceville
Tel: 02 31 24 46 11 (Yacht Club)

Type:	hard ramps to creek on Orne Estuary
Suits:	cruisers
Availability:	cruisers towards HW: smaller craft within 3hrs HW approx.
Restrictions:	national inshore speed limit
Facilities:	at ramp, parking for cars and trailers: at club, water, toilets, telephone, electricity by arrangement
Charge:	none for launching: permission from club when anyone present
Directions:	from coastal D514 take minor unsigned road through nature reserve to Base Nautique
Waters accessed:	Orne Estuary and Caen Bay

57. Ouistreham
Tel: 02 31 36 22 00 (Harbour Master)

Type:	broad, steep concrete ramp to outer harbour
Suits:	cruisers
Availability:	within 3hrs HW approx.: NB sill exists at bottom of ramp
Restrictions:	national inshore speed limit
Facilities:	very limited parking for cars and trailers on site: parking, toilets, telephones on other side of harbour, full marina services in inner yacht harbour: overnight berth for 7m, FF90
Charge:	none for launching or for access to Caen Canal
Directions:	launching site is on west side of outer harbour within sight of ferry terminal: cross canal at swing bridge and drive seawards
Waters accessed:	Caen Bay, Caen Canal and Orne Estuary

58. Coleville - Montgomery Plage

Type:	ramp to hard sand beach
Suits:	dinghies
Availability:	all states of tide but best within 3hrs HW
Restrictions:	national inshore speed limit: activity zones may be in force in summer
Facilities:	parking for cars and trailers, inshore lifeboat station, toilets
Charge:	none
Directions:	from main coast road (D514), take beach road; ramp is by ILB station
Waters accessed:	Caen Bay

59. Hermanville

Type:	ramp to hard sand beach
Suits:	dinghies
Availability:	all states of tide but best within 3hrs HW

Restrictions:	national inshore speed limit
Facilities:	parking for cars and trailers, telephone, toilets
Charge:	none
Directions:	from main coast road, take beach road; ramp is the best of a series of similar access ramps
Waters accessed:	Caen Bay

60. Le Lion-sur-Mer

Type:	ramp to hard sand beach
Suits:	dinghies
Availability:	all states of tide but best within 3hrs HW
Restrictions:	national inshore speed limit: activity zones may be in force in summer
Facilities:	parking nearby for cars and trailers, ramp is close to settlement of "Gites de Mer"; enquires to Gites de France
Charge:	none
Directions:	Lion-sur-Mer is on coastal D514; ramp is found on beach road to west of town
Waters accessed:	Caen Bay

61. Bernieres-sur-Mer

Type:	sandy gap to beach
Suits:	dinghies
Availability:	all states of tide but best within 3hrs HW
Restrictions:	national inshore speed limit
Facilities:	parking nearby for cars and trailers, toilets
Charge:	none
Directions:	Bernieres-sur-Mer is on main coast road: gap is at east end of sea front and is the first of a series of access points
Waters accessed:	Caen Bay

62. Courseulles-sur-Mer
Tel: 02 31 37 51 69 (Harbour Master)

Type:	ramp into outer harbour of tidal port
Suits:	cruisers
Availability:	cruisers towards HW: small craft within 3hrs HW
Restrictions:	speed limit in port, which dries completely at half tide
Facilities:	in outer harbour: parking, toilets, telephone: basic shopping in town, fuel from nearby garages: full marina services in inner lock basin: overnight berth for 7m, FF79
Charge:	none for launching
Directions:	in Courseulles, cross to west side of harbour and head for outer port: slip lies along most of west side of harbour
Waters accessed:	Caen Bay

63. Vers-sur-Mer (Gold Beach)

Type:	ramp to sand and stone beach
Suits:	dinghies; dayboats towards HW
Availability:	best within 3hrs HW
Restrictions:	national inshore speed limit
Facilities:	basic shopping in village, aid post near ramp, parking for cars and trailers
Charge:	none
Directions:	in village centre, ramp situated by lifeguard station
Waters accessed:	Caen Bay

64. Arromanches

Type:	ramp to hard beach
Suits:	dayboats
Availability:	all states of tide but best within 3hrs HW
Restrictions:	national inshore speed limit
Facilities:	basic shopping in Arromanches village, limited parking for cars and trailers, may be crowded in summer
Charge:	none
Directions:	via D514: road descends steeply into Arromanches; ramp is beside the D-Day museum
Waters accessed:	Caen Bay

65. Port-en-Bessin
Tel: 02 31 21 70 49 (Harbour Master)

Type:	concrete slips to outer and inner port
Suits:	cruisers
Availability:	cruisers towards HW or in inner basin, smaller craft within 3hrs HW approx.
Restrictions:	speed limit applies in port, outer part of which dries completely at half tide
Facilities:	parking for cars and trailers, basic shopping in town, telephones, toilets, lifeboat station, fuel from local garages, boatyards, chandlery: overnight berth from FF10 for small boats
Charge:	none for launching
Directions:	access via D514 and steep descent: ramps exist near LB station (dinghies), on west side of outer mole (cruisers) and at head of inner basin (cruisers) when not blocked by yard operations
Waters accessed:	Caen Bay

66. Omaha Beach

Type:	ramp to shingle beach
Suits:	dinghies
Availability:	best within 3hrs HW

Restrictions:	national inshore speed limit
Facilities:	parking for cars and trailers, inshore lifeboat
Charge:	none
Directions:	from D514, follow signs for Omaha Beach via narrow winding descent
Waters accessed:	Caen Bay

67. Vierville-sur-Mer

Type:	concrete ramp to shingle beach
Suits:	dinghies
Availability:	best within 3hrs HW
Restrictions:	national inshore speed limit
Facilities:	parking for cars and trailers, inshore lifeboat
Charge:	none
Directions:	from D514, follow D517 and signs for sea
Waters accessed:	Caen Bay

68. Grandcamp-Maisy
Tel: 02 31 22 63 16 (Harbour Master)

Type:	hard and slips to beach and outer harbour
Suits:	cruisers in harbour, dinghies on beach
Availability:	within 2hrs HW
Restrictions:	port dries completely at half tide: speed limit in port, national inshore speed limit off beach
Facilities:	parking, toilets, telephones, inshore lifeboat, crane, chandler, boatyard, basic shopping in town, fuel in inner basin, overnight berth for 7m, FF55
Charge:	none for launching
Directions:	situated on D514: slips to beach are at east end of town near ILB station; cruiser slips are to west of outer basin with access from car and boat park
Waters accessed:	Caen Bay

69. Isigny
Tel: 02 31 22 10 67 (Harbour Master)

Type:	half-tide slip
Suits:	cruisers
Availability:	cruisers towards HW, smaller craft within 2-3hrs HW
Restrictions:	national inshore speed limit
Facilities:	parking for cars and trailers: in yacht harbour, toilets, telephones, water, fuel, crane available; overnight berths: enquire harbour master, shopping in town centre
Charge:	none for launching
Directions:	access via N13/E46 motorway: follow signs for Isigny; slip is on east side of port in town centre, 400m from main road near boatyard
Waters accessed:	Carentan Bay and Channel

70. Le Grand Vey

Type:	half-tide slip
Suits:	cruisers
Availability:	cruisers towards HW, smaller craft to half tide
Restrictions:	national inshore speed limit
Facilities:	parking for cars and trailers, 50m
Charge:	none
Directions:	map reading skill helps! From N13/E46, take D913 to Ste Marie le Mont, then D115 to this small village
Waters accessed:	Carentan Bay and Channel

71. Quineville

Type:	gaps in dunes and concrete ramp to hard beach
Suits:	dinghies
Availability:	within 2hrs HW approx.
Restrictions:	national inshore speed limit: activity zones may be in force
Facilities:	parking for cars and trailers, may be crowded in summer, basic supplies, telephone in village
Charge:	none
Directions:	from N13/E3/E46 at Montebourg, take D42 to Quineville: best beach access is to north of sea front by Musee de la Liberte
Waters accessed:	Channel

72. St Vaast-la-Hougue
Tel: 02 33 23 61 00 (Harbour Master)

Type:	concrete slip outside harbour
Suits:	cruisers
Availability:	cruisers towards HW, smaller craft as soon as flats covered
Restrictions:	national inshore speed limit, numerous oyster layings must be avoided
Facilities:	at slip: parking for cars and trailers: in town, basic shopping, telephones: fuel from local garage: in yacht harbour, water, toilets, fuel, crane: overnight berth for 7m, FF69
Charge:	none for launching
Directions:	from Valognes, take D902 to Quettenou, then D1: slip is on north side of harbour, outside mole, near boat park
Waters accessed:	Channel

73. Reville

Type:	sandy gaps to beach
Suits:	dinghies
Availability:	within 3hrs HW approx.
Restrictions:	national inshore speed limit: avoid oyster layings
Facilities:	parking for cars and trailers nearby

Charge:	none
Directions:	from D902, via D328 following signs for Reville and continuing to sea
Waters accessed:	Saire Bay and Channel

74. Landemer

Type:	ramp giving access to cove
Suits:	dinghies
Availability:	within 3hrs HW approx.
Restrictions:	national inshore speed limit
Facilities:	basic parking for cars and trailers
Charge:	none
Directions:	from D902, via D10 to La Crasvillerie, then coastal D1 to Landemer village, where access will be found direct from coast road
Waters accessed:	Channel

75. Barfleur
Tel: 02 33 54 08 29 (Harbour Master - part time)

Type:	slips to drying harbour and beach
Suits:	cruisers
Availability:	cruisers within 2hrs HW, small craft when water in harbour
Restrictions:	speed limit in port, which dries out completely
Facilities:	parking for cars and trailers, telephones, toilets, inshore lifeboat, water, fuel from local garages: basic shopping in town centre: overnight berth for 7m, FF38
Charge:	none for launching
Directions:	from Cherbourg follow D901 to Barfleur: in port, first small slip is at south end of harbourside road: other slips near ILB station; one for dinghies to beach, one to half-tide for cruisers - this is sometimes obstructed
Waters accessed:	Channel

76. Gatteville

Type:	unmade approach road to cove
Suits:	dinghies
Availability:	within 2hrs HW approx.
Restrictions:	national inshore speed limit
Facilities:	limited wild parking for cars and trailers
Charge:	none
Directions:	off D901, via D10 towards lighthouse: a wild and secret site within sight of the Pointe de Barfleur and well worth the effort!
Waters accessed:	Channel

77. La Hogue / La Hoguette

Type:	beach launching
Suits:	dinghies
Availability:	all states of tide
Restrictions:	national inshore speed limit
Facilities:	wild parking for cars and trailers
Charge:	none
Directions:	via D901 and D10, just beyond Gatteville: another completely wild site
Waters accessed:	Channel

78. Le Bequet

Type:	slip to drying harbour
Suits:	cruisers
Availability:	cruisers on tide, small craft within 2hrs HW approx.
Restrictions:	national inshore speed limit
Facilities:	parking for cars and trailers, inshore lifeboat, telephone nearby: all other facilities in Cherbourg
Charge:	none
Directions:	from Cherbourg, take coastal D116 to this largely forgotten fishing harbour: slip near ILB station
Waters accessed:	Channel

79. Cherbourg
Tel: 02 33 87 65 70 (Marina Harbour Master)

All facilities within the port of Cherbourg are geared to larger cruising yachts, and civil and military traffic may be intense. Further information re berthing and traffic restrictions should be sought from the marina: all small craft launching facilities are to the west of the commercial and naval port

Type:	ramps to Outer Harbour
Suits:	cruisers
Availability:	cruisers within 2hrs HW, small craft all states of tide
Restrictions:	speed limit and traffic restrictions apply in port: obtain local information from cruising almanac
Facilities:	parking for cars and trailers
Charge:	none
Directions:	from Cherbourg take coastal D901 west to Hameau de la Mer: on seaward side of road are fishermen's and anglers' car parks; a series of ramps, the most westward of which is suitable for cruisers, gives access to the outer harbour
Waters accessed:	Grande Rade and Channel

80. La Riviere

Type:	beach launching and half-tide ramp
Suits:	beach launching for dinghies, ramp for cruisers
Availability:	cruisers at HW, small craft within 3hrs HW approx.
Restrictions:	national inshore speed limit
Facilities:	parking for cars and trailers, water, toilets at nearby sailing club
Charge:	none
Directions:	from coastal D901 via D22 to La Riviere, where turn right at Rue de Nez to fort: beach launching to right of fort for dinghies; ramp on far side, near cannon and lifeboat station
Waters accessed:	Channel

81. Omonville-La-Rogue

Type:	ramp to tidal harbour
Suits:	cruisers
Availability:	cruisers within 1-2hrs HW, small craft within 4hrs HW
Restrictions:	national inshore speed limit
Facilities:	parking for cars and trailers, telephone, toilets, basic local shopping
Charge:	none
Directions:	Omonville-la-Rogue is on the D45: two ramps exist, the larger of which is behind the breakwater
Waters accessed:	Channel

82. Goury

Type:	ramp into tidal harbour
Suits:	dayboats
Availability:	within 3hrs HW approx.
Restrictions:	national inshore speed limit: lifeboat launching area to be kept clear
Facilities:	parking for cars and trailers, toilets, water, telephone
Charge:	none
Directions:	Goury is at the end of D901: slips situated close to lifeboat slip
Waters accessed:	Channel

83. Dielette
Tel: 02 33 53 68 78 (Harbour Master)

Type:	ramp into tidal harbour
Suits:	cruisers
Availability:	cruisers towards HW, smaller craft within 3hrs HW
Restrictions:	harbour dries completely at half-tide: speed limit in port
Facilities:	by launching site: parking for cars and trailers: in inner port: water, electricity, toilets, telephones, fuel, overnight berth for 7m, FF80

Charge:	none for launching in 1997
Directions:	from D904, take D23 following signs for Le Port: slips situated at south end of outer harbour
Waters accessed:	Channel

84. Sciotot

Type:	ramp to beach
Suits:	dinghies
Availability:	within 3hrs HW
Restrictions:	national inshore speed limit: activity zones may be in force in summer
Facilities:	parking for cars and trailers, may be crowded in summer, toilets, rescue station, inshore lifeboat, water, telephone nearby
Charge:	none
Directions:	from D904 at Les Pieux, follow D4 and minor coast road to Anse de Sciotot
Waters accessed:	Sciotot Bay

85. Carteret
Tel: 02 33 04 70 84 (Harbour Master)

Type:	slip to hard sand
Suits:	cruisers
Availability:	within 2hrs HW approx.
Restrictions:	speed limit in port: whole harbour dries at half-tide
Facilities:	at launch site: parking for cars and trailers: nearby, lifeboat, telephone, toilets; in yacht basin, water, electricity, fuel from nearby garages, chandler in town, basic shopping, overnight berth for 7m, FF70
Charge:	none for launching
Directions:	turn off D904 to Barneville-Carteret, follow signs for Le Port and continue seaward past yacht harbour to outer harbour and car park
Waters accessed:	Channel

86. Portbail

Type:	ramp to hard sand
Suits:	cruisers
Availability:	cruisers towards HW, smaller craft within 2hrs HW approx.
Restrictions:	speed limit applies in port: whole port dries out at half-tide
Facilities:	by launching site: parking for car and trailer: at yacht basin (drying), telephones, toilets, water; fuel from local garages, shopping in town centre
Charge:	none
Directions:	from D903, take D50 to Portbail and follow signs for Le Port: launching site is on creek upstream of yacht basin
Waters accessed:	Channel

87. Agon-Coutainville

Type:	ramps to beach
Suits:	dayboats
Availability:	within 2hrs HW approx.
Restrictions:	national inshore speed limit
Facilities:	parking for cars and trailers, telephone, shopping in town centre, fuel from local garages
Charge:	none
Directions:	from Coutances via D44, follow signs for sea: first ramp to beach from sea front, second by lighthouse; third, lit at night, where road turns to Pointe d'Agon; small sailing club nearby
Waters accessed:	Channel

88. Regneville-sur-Mer

Type:	hard giving access to estuary
Suits:	light-draught cruisers
Availability:	cruisers towards HW, small craft within 2hrs HW approx.
Restrictions:	national inshore speed limit
Facilities:	parking for cars and trailers, nearby boatyard, garage, telephone, basic shopping in village
Charge:	none
Directions:	from Coutances via D20 and D49
Waters accessed:	Sienne Estuary andChannel

89. Haire-de-la-Vanlee

Type:	beach launching
Suits:	dinghies
Availability:	within 1hr HW approx.
Restrictions:	national inshore speed limit
Facilities:	limited parking for cars and trailers
Charge:	none
Directions:	from D971, take D98 as for St Martin via Bricqueville-sur-Mer: road leads via ford at Les Salines - **caution** recommended; at Haire-de-la-Vanlee, launch dinghies seaward side over beach
Waters accessed:	Channel

90. Granville
Tel: 02 33 50 20 06 (Marina Harbour Master)

Type:	slips to drying harbour
Suits:	cruisers
Availability:	towards HW; **note** that the whole area dries
Restrictions:	speed limit in port: **caution** required during ferry movements
Facilities:	parking for cars and trailers, nearby telephones, chandlery, boatyard: in yacht harbour, fuel, cranes, showers, toilets, elec-

	tricity, water, shopping in town centre, fuel from local garages, overnight berth for 7m, FF76
Charge:	none for launching
Directions:	on entering port complex, proceed to seaward side: broad half-tide slip to soft mud near Halle de Poissons; a further ramp suitable for dinghies exists beyond Port de Plaisance, but care should be taken of its half-tide sill protecting a saltwater swimming pool
Waters accessed:	Iles Chausey and Baie de Mont St. Michel

91. Mont St. Michel

Note: Although two launching sites for dinghies existed here until 1997, they are now condemned by major works intended to return Mont St. Michel to its former island status, and it is at present uncertain what facilities may exist here for small boats when these works are eventually completed

The Channel to the Med
A Guide to the Main Routes through the French Canals
ISBN 1-898574-03-0

by

Derek Bowskill

The acknowledged guide to voyaging through the French inland waterways to the Mediterranean

£19.95
+£1.50 p&p

Written by a well-known writer and French waterway enthusiast this book with its lively and informative text, accompanied by over 80 maps illustrating the routes and showing locks, stopping places, hazards and other points of interest gives detailed coverage of the main inland routes from the Channel to the Mediterranean. General information on choice of routes, gear, regulations, licences and practical hints on methods of locking are given in chapter 1, with subsequent chapters covering the routes in detail. A comprehensive index gives immedite access to over 600 places en-route and tabulated information at the beginning of thebook puts information on distances, number of locks, headroom and water depths at your fingertips.

available from: Bookshops and Yacht Chandlers or the Publishers,
OPUS Book Publishing Limited
20 East Road, West Mersea, Colchester, Essex.CO5 8EB
Tel / Fax: 01206 383629 e-mail: opus@dmac.co.uk
Credit cards accepted

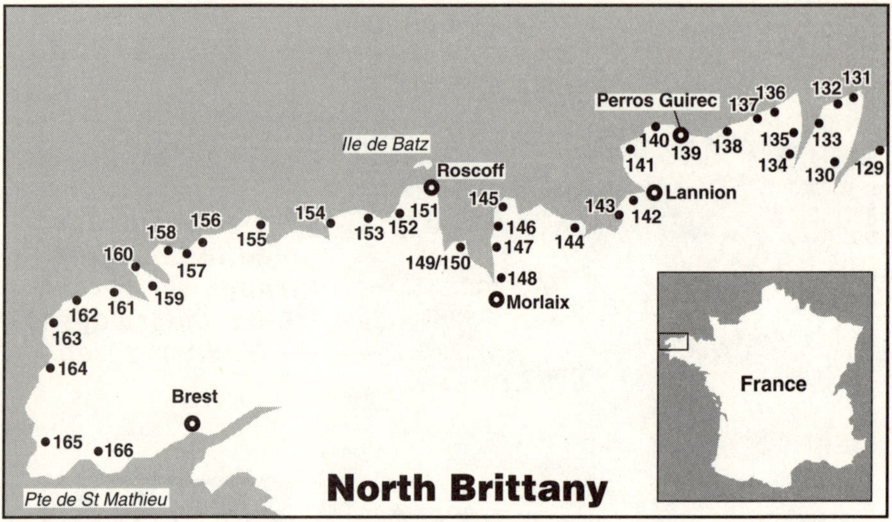
Perros Guirec
131
132
136
137
133
135
138
140
139
134
130
129
141
Lannion
Ile de Batz
Roscoff
145
143
142
151
154
152
153
156
146
158
155
147
144
160
149/150
157
148
159
Morlaix
161
162
163
164
Brest
165
166
Pte de St Mathieu
North Brittany
France

92. Cherrueix

Type: beach landing
Suits: dinghies
Availability: within 1hr HW approx.
Restrictions: national inshore speed limit: **caution**: offshore mussel stakes exist along the whole of this coast
Facilities: parking for cars and trailers and yacht hire nearby, toilets, basic shopping in village
Charge: none
Directions: from the N176 at Dol-de-Bretagne, take D4 and D155 to Le Vivier-sur-Mer then D797 east to Cherrueix village and follow signs for beach
Waters accessed: Bay of Mont St. Michel

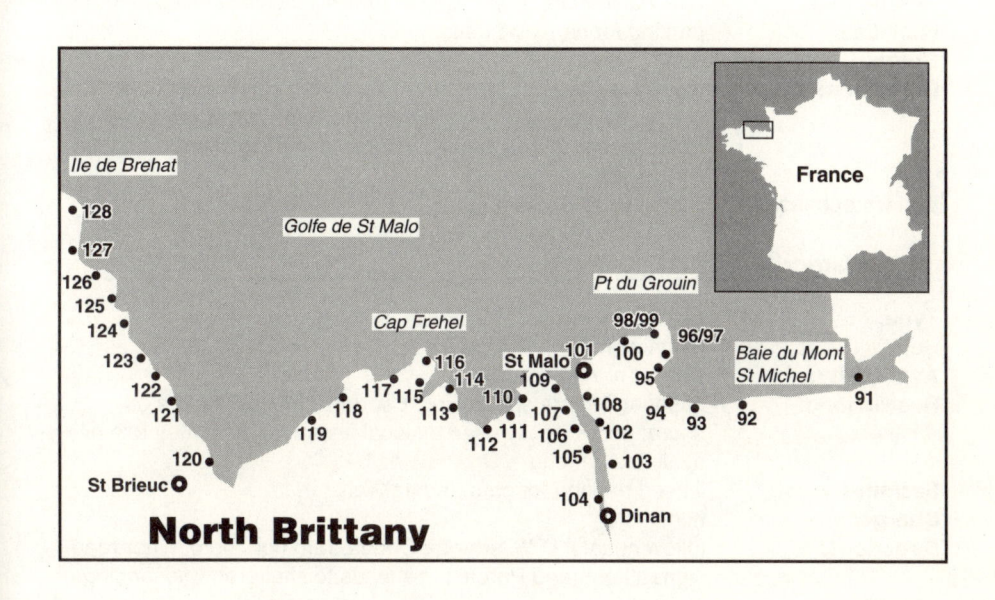

North Brittany

93. Le Vivier-sur-Mer

Type:	broad slip to creek
Suits:	cruisers
Availability:	cruisers at HW, small craft within 1hr HW
Restrictions:	**caution** - mussel stakes offshore: fishermen have priority
Facilities:	parking for cars and trailers, telephone at nearby Gare Maritime
Charge:	none
Directions:	from the N176 at Dol-de-Bretagne, take D4 and D155 to Le Vivier village: public area of port is first part entered, beyond which access restricted to fishermen
Waters accessed:	Bay of Mont St. Michel

94. Hirel

Type:	beach landing
Suits:	dinghies
Availability:	within 1hr HW approx.
Restrictions:	national inshore speed limit: **caution** - mussel stakes offshore
Facilities:	parking for cars and trailers
Charge:	none
Directions:	follow coastal D155 west from Le Vivier: at Hirel village a series of wild launching sites, simply gaps in roadside marram grass, begin. A delightfully unspoilt launching site for dinghies on the tide
Waters accessed:	Bay of Mont St. Michel

95. Le Grand Porcan

Type:	beach landing
Suits:	dinghies
Availability:	within 1hr HW approx.
Restrictions:	national inshore speed limit: **caution** - mussel stakes offshore: occasionally used by local fishermen who may use all available parking
Facilities:	limited parking for cars and trailers
Charge:	none
Directions:	follow coastal D76: after La Coudre turn right onto minor road signed Le Grand Porcan; this leads to sheltered wild landing in small bay
Waters accessed:	Bay of Mont St. Michel

96. Cancale

Type:	series of slips to drying harbour
Suits:	cruisers (largest slip)
Availability:	cruisers within 2hrs HW: small craft within 4hrs HW
Restrictions:	speed limit applies in harbour: fishermen have priority at slips
Facilities:	parking for cars and trailers may be crowded in summer, telephones, toilets, water point, fuel from garage in town, information office, nearby boatyard, shopping in town and at St Malo
Charge:	none
Directions:	at Cancale, follow signs for sea: steep descent leads to beach and harbour where a series of dinghy slips are followed, near fish market, by the main slip which is practicable for vehicles and leads to hard sand
Waters accessed:	Bay of Mont St. Michel

97. Greve de Port Briac

Type:	slip to hard sand in cove
Suits:	dinghies; dayboats launched by 4x4 vehicles
Availability:	all states of tide
Restrictions:	national inshore speed limit
Facilities:	parking for cars and trailers
Charge:	none
Directions:	from Cancale town centre, follow coastal D201 and signs for Greve de Port Briac: road descends direct to ramp near former pilot station
Waters accessed:	Bay of Mont St. Michel and Channel

98. Port Pican

Type:	slip to cove
Suits:	dayboats
Availability:	dayboats within 3hrs HW, dinghies all states of tide
Restrictions:	national inshore speed limit
Facilities:	parking for cars and trailers, nearby telephone, toilets, water at sailing club when open
Charge:	none
Directions:	from Cancale, follow coastal D201 and minor road signed for Port Pican: steep descent leads to cove with slip, green parking and small sailing club
Waters accessed:	Bay of Mont St. Michel and Channel

99. Port Mer

Type:	slip to beach in cove
Suits:	dinghies
Availability:	all states of tide
Restrictions:	national inshore speed limit
Facilities:	parking for cars and trailers, may be crowded in summer, toilets, telephone, bicycle hire, nearby campsite
Charge:	none
Directions:	follow D201 from Cancale, and take minor road signed for Port Mer: **caution** - very steep descent leads to beach with ramp to hard sand
Waters accessed:	Bay of Mont St. Michel and Channel

100. Havre de Rotheneuf

Type:	ramp to hard beach
Suits:	dinghies
Availability:	all states of tide
Restrictions:	national inshore speed limit
Facilities:	limited parking for cars and trailers

Charge:	none
Directions:	follow coastal D201 Cancale - St Malo, and take minor road signed for Havre de Rotheneuf, leading to semi-landlocked bay
Waters accessed:	Bay of Mont St. Michel and Channel

101. St Malo
Tel: 02 99 56 60 02 (Administration)

Type:	series of slips to harbour or Rance Estuary (1) Cale du Naye (2) Cale de la Capitainerie (3) Tour Solidor
Suits:	cruisers
Availability:	half-tide: small craft at all states of tide at (3)
Restrictions:	speed limits apply in port: half-tide sill obstructs access to and from yacht basin. **Caution:** be aware of ferry and commercial shipping movements; commercial shipping has right of way
Facilities:	parking for cars and trailers may be crowded in summer at sites other than (1). Facilities in yacht harbour (Port des Sablons) include toilets, showers, water and electricity on pontoons, fuel from pumps on pontoons (NB assistance needed as pumps work on French credit cards only), nearby boatyard, sailmaker, marine engineer: overnight berth for 7m Port des Sablons FF85, old town port FF63. Facilities in St Malo and neighbouring St Servan include shopping, fuel from local garages, excellent tourist information etc.
Charge:	none for launching at public slips: parking of boats and cars in Port des Sablons may be subject to charge
Directions:	(1) Cale du Naye: follow signs for car ferries, turning left as for Fort Naye and launch from free car park into yacht basin protected by half-tide sill (2) Cale de la Capitainerie: follow signs for Port des Sablons and launch into yacht basin: a charge may be made for larger craft (3) Tour Solidor: follow signs from St Malo centre to St Servan, then for Port St Pere: two slips exist by Tour Solidor
Waters accessed:	Rade de St Malo, Rance Estuary and Channel

102. St Suliac

Type:	concrete slip to estuary
Suits:	cruisers
Availability:	cruisers at HW, small craft at all states of tide
Restrictions:	speed limits apply in river
Facilities:	parking for cars and trailers, toilets, water, telephones, electricity by arrangement on site, basic shopping in town centre, sailing club when open
Charge:	none
Directions:	from St Malo, take N137 south, then D117 for St Suliac town: main street descends to estuary
Waters accessed:	Rance Estuary, Channel and Breton canals

103. Mordreuc

Type:	slip to estuary
Suits:	cruisers
Availability:	cruisers towards HW, small craft at all states of tide except dead LW
Restrictions:	speed limits apply in river
Facilities:	parking for cars and trailers, fuel from nearby garage, telephone in nearby bar
Charge:	none
Directions:	from St Malo, take N137 south, then minor roads for Pleudihen and D48 to Mordreuc: main street leads to estuary and slip
Waters accessed:	Rance Estuary, Channel and Breton canals

104. Lyvet le Port

Type:	slip to canalised section of River Rance
Suits:	cruisers with care
Availability:	unlimited
Restrictions:	speed limits apply
Facilities:	parking nearby for cars and trailers, telephone, toilets, basic shopping in village, fuel from yacht basin
Charge:	none: note no licence required (1998) for Breton waterways
Directions:	from N137, via D676 and D29, following signs for Lyvet le Port: slip is at upstream end of port on right bank, beyond parking area
Waters accessed:	Breton waterways

105. Plage du Roue

Type:	hard foreshore for launching
Suits:	dayboats
Availability:	all states of tide except dead LW
Restrictions:	speed limit applies in river
Facilities:	parking for cars and trailers
Charge:	none
Directions:	from N176/E401 motorway, take D12 north through Langrolay and follow signs on minor roads for Plage du Roue
Waters accessed:	Rance Estuary and Breton waterways

106. La Jouvente

Type:	steep slip to estuary
Suits:	cruisers
Availability:	all states of tide
Restrictions:	speed limit applies in river
Facilities:	parking for cars and trailers, may be crowded in summer,

Charge:	none
Directions:	water on quay on D114 (left bank of Rance) follow signs for La Jouvente down steep descent past Jersey Lillie pub to slip
Waters accessed:	Rance Estuary and Breton Waterways

107. Port La Richardais

Type:	hard giving access to creek and Rance Estuary
Suits:	dayboats
Availability:	towards HW
Restrictions:	speed limit applies in river
Facilities:	parking for cars and trailers, water, boatyard
Charge:	none
Directions:	from St Malo, cross Rance Barrage and take D114: at La Richardais, take minor side road to creek
Waters accessed:	Rance Estuary and Breton waterways

108. Rance Barrage

Type:	half-tide ramp to waiting area for tidal lock
Suits:	cruisers: **caution:** - in some conditions, weed can grow on this slip to a dangerous extent: it is advisable to make prior investigation on foot
Availability:	within 3hrs HW
Restrictions:	speed limit applies in river: obtain local information on lock opening times; keep clear of safety boom in vicinity of Rance Barrage
Facilities:	parking for cars and trailers, telephone, toilets in cruise boat terminal nearby. Guided tours of tidal power station during daytime working hours: telephone information line (in French) on lock operating hours on 02 99 16 37 13
Charge:	none
Directions:	follow signs from St Malo
Waters accessed:	Rance Estuary above and below lock

109. Dinard, Clair de la Lune

Type:	long full-tide slip to Rance Estuary
Suits:	cruisers with care
Availability:	all states of tide except LWS
Restrictions:	fishermen have priority: speed limit applies inshore; care required as tide flows across slip and may be hazardous in some conditions
Facilities:	limited parking at head of slip and nearby for cars and trailers: under no circumstances park on slip owing to great range of tide - some fools occasionally do! Shopping, telephones etc. in Dinard town centre, inshore lifeboat station

Charge:	none
Directions:	in Dinard town, make for northern end (Clair de la Lune) and follow winding waterside roadway to slip
Waters accessed:	Rance Estuary and Rade de St Malo

110. St Briac-sur-Mer

Type:	hard foreshore launching
Suits:	dayboats
Availability:	larger craft towards HW, dinghies at all states of tide
Restrictions:	national inshore speed limit: beware bait diggers' holes
Facilities:	parking for cars and trailers, telephone
Charge:	none
Directions:	from Dinard, take coastal D786 and turn seaward at traffic lights: two slips lead to hard foreshore
Waters accessed:	Fremur River and Channel

111. Le Rieul

Type:	hard foreshore
Suits:	dayboats
Availability:	larger craft towards HW, dinghies at all states of tide
Restrictions:	national inshore speed limit
Facilities:	parking for cars and trailers, nearby boatyard
Charge:	none
Directions:	following coastal D786 south from St Briac, just after Fremur bridge take minor road past boatyard down to foreshore
Waters accessed:	Fremur River and Channel

112. St Jacut de la Mer

Type:	steep ramp to harbour sands
Suits:	dinghies
Availability:	within 3hrs HW approx.
Restrictions:	national inshore speed limit: activity zones nearby in summer
Facilities:	very limited roadside parking, telephone in former coast lookout
Charge:	none
Directions:	continue along coastal D786 to St-Jacut de la Mer: here follow coast road to minor road leading down (steep descent) to Port du Chatelet, where steep ramp with hauling rings gives access to small harbour
Waters accessed:	Channel

113. Notre Dame du Guildo

Type:	slips to estuary of River Arguenon
Suits:	cruisers
Availability:	cruisers; towards HW, smaller craft within 2hrs HW

Restrictions:	national inshore speed limit
Facilities:	parking nearby for cars and trailers, may be crowded in summer
Charge:	none
Directions:	from coastal D786, at Notre Dame du Guildo, follow minor road to port: two slips exist, the larger and the only one suitable for cruisers is on the right bank
Waters accessed:	River Arguenon and Channel

114. St Cast le Guildo, Port Jacquet

Type:	slip to hard sand of tidal harbour
Suits:	cruisers
Availability:	cruisers towards HW, small craft over sands at any state of tide
Restrictions:	speed limit applies in harbour
Facilities:	parking for cars and trailers may be crowded in summer, telephone, toilets, waterpoint, basic shopping in village, two chandlers nearby
Charge:	none in 1997; local council reported to be considering charging
Directions:	from D786, follow signs for St Cast le Guildo, where road descends steep hill to port: quayside has one-way system in force and launching ramp leads from this to harbour. There is a better ramp in fishing port but fishermen have priority
Waters accessed:	Channel

115. Port Nieux

Type:	ramp to head of creek
Suits:	cruisers
Availability:	cruisers towards HW, smaller craft within 2hrs HW
Restrictions:	national inshore speed limit
Facilities:	parking for cars and trailers
Charge:	none
Directions:	from St Cast take D786 to D16, which leads to Port Nieux, now a disused former coaster quay: slip from quayside gives access to 2m water MHW
Waters accessed:	Baie de la Frenaye

116. Pleheral Plage

Type:	half-tide ramp giving access to cove
Suits:	dayboats
Availability:	within 3hrs HW approx.
Restrictions:	national inshore speed limit
Facilities:	parking for cars and trailers; **note** one-way system; nearby camp site
Charge:	none
Directions:	from D786, turn north onto D34 at Frehel following signs for

	Pleherel Plage. Here at Anse du Croc, steep ramp leads out over rocks at Pointe aux Chevres
Waters accessed:	Channel

117. Pointe du Champ du Port

Type:	concrete ramp to hard sand in tidal harbour
Suits:	dayboats
Availability:	within 3hrs HW approx.
Restrictions:	national inshore speed limit, nearest parking by permit, beware of bait diggers' holes in sand
Facilities:	parking for cars and trailers 200m (permit only), telephone at nearby municipal camp site
Charge:	none for launching
Directions:	access from D786, following signs for Pointe du Champ du Port
Waters accessed:	Channel

118. Erquy
Tel: 02 96 72 19 32 (Harbour Master)

Type:	broad half-tide slip to drying harbour
Suits:	cruisers
Availability:	cruisers within 2hrs HW: small craft launch over sand at any state of tide
Restrictions:	speed limit applies in port: fishermen have priority at slips
Facilities:	near slip, parking for cars and trailers, telephone, toilets, water: electricity by arrangement with HM, crane, boatyard, chandler. Overnight berth in drying harbour for 7m, FF33
Charge:	none for launching
Directions:	Erquy is reached from coastal D786: signposting in town is extremely poor. When port eventually found, parking area is behind Bureau du Port, with slip nearby
Waters accessed:	Baie de St Brieuc

119. Ville Berneuf

Type:	ramp to hard sand beach
Suits:	dinghies
Availability:	any state of tide, but best towards HW
Restrictions:	national inshore speed limit
Facilities:	parking for cars and trailers
Charge:	none
Directions:	from Erquy, follow D786 towards St Brieuc: turn right at roundabout following signs for Ville Berneuf; road leads direct to beach
Waters accessed:	Baie de St Brieuc

120. St Brieuc - Port de Legue
Tel: 02 96 62 70 22 (Harbour Master)

Type:	slip to outer harbour of tidal port
Suits:	cruisers
Availability:	within 2hrs HW
Restrictions:	speed limit applies in port: commercial shipping has priority; whole outer area dries towards LW
Facilities:	near slip: parking for cars and trailers. In inner port: boatyards, water, toilets, showers, telephone. Crane available, chandler, fuel from nearby garage, basic shopping nearby, overnight berth for 7m, FF43
Charge:	none for launching into outer harbour
Directions:	from St Brieuc, follow signs from main N12 for Port du Legue. When in Legue, outer slip is at seaward end of right, or east, bank of outer port: all other facilities to be found in inner port
Waters accessed:	Baie de St Brieuc

121. Binic
Tel: 02 96 73 61 86 (Harbour Master)

Type:	slips to hard sand in drying outer harbour
Suits:	cruisers
Availability:	within 3hrs HW
Restrictions:	speed limit applies in port: beware moorings in outer harbour; **note** whole area dries at LW. Major works in yacht harbour planned for 1998: advisable to investigate first
Facilities:	parking for cars and trailers, telephone, toilets, showers, two chandlers, fuel from garages in town, crane available. Overnight berth for 7m, from FF30
Charge:	none for launching
Directions:	from St Brieuc, take N12, follow signs for Paimpol on D786. In Binic, follow signs for port: two slips available, best on right bank near yacht club, another for smaller craft at corner of north side of outer port on Quai Surcouf
Waters accessed:	Baie de St Brieuc

122. St Quay Portrieux
Tel: 02 96 70 81 30 (Harbour Master)

Type:	slip to drying outer harbour
Suits:	cruisers
Availability:	cruisers towards HW, smaller craft within 3hrs HW
Restrictions:	speed limit applies in port: parking area may be obstructed on Mondays by market stalls; whole area dries at half-tide
Facilities:	near launching site in Portrieux: parking for cars and trailers, chandler, toilets, showers, water, basic shopping, telephone nearby, inshore lifeboat station. In yacht harbour: water on pon-

	toons, toilets, telephone, fuel, crane. Overnight berth for 7m, from FF48
Charge:	none for launching
Directions:	from coastal D786, enter Portrieux where all facilities are situated: there is no quay at St Quay. Launching sites are in old drying port: series of ramps from Quai de la Republique lead down to hard sand
Waters accessed:	Baie de St Brieuc

123. Greve St Marc

Type:	ramp to beach in cove
Suits:	dinghies
Availability:	all states of tide
Restrictions:	national inshore speed limit
Facilities:	parking for cars and trailers, emergency telephone
Charge:	none
Directions:	from D786, follow signs first for Port Goret, then, at T junction, for Viver and Greve St Marc
Waters accessed:	Baie de St Brieuc and Channel

124. Plage de Palus

Type:	concrete ramp to hard beach
Suits:	dayboats
Availability:	any state of tide
Restrictions:	national inshore speed limit: activity zones in force in summer
Facilities:	parking for cars and trailers, water, telephone in restaurant
Charge:	none
Directions:	from D786, at Plouha, follow signs, via D32, for Palus-Plage
Waters accessed:	Baie de St Brieuc and Channel

125. Brehec

Type:	concrete ramp to hard beach
Suits:	dinghies
Availability:	any state of tide
Restrictions:	national inshore speed limit: care required among crowded moorings in cove
Facilities:	parking for cars and trailers, telephone, toilets
Charge:	none
Directions:	from D786, take D54 for Brehec at Lanloup: follow signs for plage, leading to cove
Waters accessed:	Channel

126. Port Lazo

Type:	ramp to hard sand beach
Suits:	dinghies
Availability:	all states of tide except dead LW
Restrictions:	national inshore speed limit: care required - oyster layings
Facilities:	limited parking for cars and trailers, telephone, toilets
Charge:	none
Directions:	from coastal D54 to north of Brehec plage, take D77 to Port Lazo; beach is short distance past Cap Horn camp site
Waters accessed:	Channel

127. Paimpol
Tel; 02 96 20 80 77 (Harbour Master)

Type:	slip to drying outer harbour
Suits:	cruisers
Availability:	cruisers within 2hrs HW, smaller craft within 3hrs HW
Restrictions:	speed limit applies in port: **Caution:** busy fishing port; whole outer area dries at half tide
Facilities:	near launch site: parking for cars and trailers, chandler, boatyard, marine engineer. In inner port: water and electricity on pontoons, toilets, showers, telephones, fuel, crane available. Overnight berth for 7m, FF88
Charge:	none for launching
Directions:	Paimpol is reached via coastal D786. In Paimpol town, launch sites are on right or south side of outer harbour, past Customs. Port Office and tidal lock. Concrete slip is usable by trailed craft of any size: another slip exists at seaward end of opposite side but is usable towards HW only
Waters accessed:	Channel

128. Pors Even

Type:	ramp to drying harbour
Suits:	cruisers
Availability:	all states of tide
Restrictions:	fishermen have priority: speed limit applies in port
Facilities:	parking for cars and trailers at New Harbour; toilets, water, telephone
Charge:	none
Directions:	from Paimpol, follow D789 north, taking minor road to Perros Hamon and Pors Even: main street leads to harbour
Waters accessed:	Anse de Paimpol and Channel

129. Loguivy-sur-Mer

Type:	concrete ramp to hard beach in drying harbour
Suits:	cruisers
Availability:	cruisers within 2hrs HW, smaller craft at any state of tide
Restrictions:	fishermen have priority: speed limit applies in port
Facilities:	parking for cars and trailers, toilets, water, telephone nearby, inshore lifeboat station, fuel from local garage or on local jetty when anyone present to assist from fishing co-operative, basic shopping only
Charge:	none
Directions:	from Paimpol, take D789 north then minor D15 to Loguivy: local signposting poor - good map reading skills essential! In port, leisure craft launch from ramp on left side of harbour
Waters accessed:	Trieux Estuary and Channel

130. Lezardrieux
Tel: 02 96 20 14 22 (Harbour Master)

Type:	broad slip to hard beach
Suits:	cruisers
Availability:	cruisers within 1hr HW, smaller craft within 3hrs HW
Restrictions:	speed limit applies in port: care required among moorings
Facilities:	near slip, water point, telephone, parking nearby, chandler, sailmaker in town. In yacht harbour, water and electricity, showers, toilets, fuel. Overnight berth for 7m, FF60
Charge:	none for launching
Directions:	Lezardrieux is on D786. In town, follow signs for port: slip and hard are to left of pontoon berths
Waters accessed:	Trieux Estuary and Channel

131. Larmor

Type:	launching across hard shingle to cove
Suits:	cruisers
Availability:	cruisers towards HW, small craft any state of tide
Restrictions:	national inshore speed limit
Facilities:	parking for cars and trailers by roadside, telephone in village square
Charge:	none
Directions:	from Lezardrieux take D20 northwards, then D33 following signs for L'Armor. Here follow signs for CEVA via Rue des Goemoniers (wrack gatherers): park on road and launch over shingle
Waters accessed:	Iles de Brehat, Trieux Estuary and Channel

132. Port de la Chaine

Type:	cove landing
Suits:	dinghies
Availability:	all states of tide but best within 3hrs HW
Restrictions:	national inshore speed limit
Facilities:	parking for cars and trailers
Charge:	none
Directions:	this wild and largely secret site is found west of Larmor. From the D20 turn north at St Antoine onto a badly signed minor road leading to a former coastguard lookout above the cove
Waters accessed:	Channel and Jaudy Estuary

133. Port Beni

Type:	launch over hard shingle
Suits:	dayboats
Availability:	within 1hr HW
Restrictions:	national inshore speed limit: parking prohibited on approach road; foreshore is nature reserve
Facilities:	parking for cars and trailers on rough quay, toilets, water point
Charge:	none
Directions:	from D20, via minor, badly signed roads to Jaudy Estuary
Waters accessed:	Jaudy Estuary and Channel

134. Treguier
Tel: 02 96 92 42 37 (Harbour Master)

Type:	narrow slip to drying sector of port
Suits:	dayboats
Availability:	within 1hr HW
Restrictions:	speed limit applies in port. **Caution:** coasters regularly enter and leave river; care should be taken to avoid oyster layings
Facilities:	parking for cars and trailers, water point, toilets, chandler nearby, basic shopping in town. Overnight berth for 7m, FF77
Charge:	none for launching (1997)
Directions:	Treguier is reached via the D786 and the yacht harbour is seen on west side of river near bridge: slip is beyond the dinghy park
Waters accessed:	Jaudy Estuary

135. La Roche Jaune

Type:	ramp to hard beach
Suits:	cruisers
Availability:	cruisers within 2hrs HW, small craft within 3hrs HW
Restrictions:	national inshore speed limit
Facilities:	parking for cars and trailers

Charge:	none
Directions:	from Treguier, take road north to Plougrescant then turn right onto D8 and follow signs for La Roche Jaune, where two ramps exist, one to hard beach, one to half-tide sill by quay
Waters accessed:	Jaudy Estuary

136. Pors Scaff

Type:	slip to semi-landlocked bay
Suits:	dayboats
Availability:	within 2hrs HW
Restrictions:	national inshore speed limit applies in whole of bay
Facilities:	parking for cars and trailers
Charge:	none
Directions:	this wild and extremely interesting site is reached via minor roads from Plougrescant village. Note that wild camping is forbidden (conservation area) but sleeping aboard light-draught cruisers is not, making this bay an attractive overnight anchorage for boats which will take the ground
Waters accessed:	Channel

137. Port Blanc

Type:	slips to hard beach
Suits:	dayboats
Availability:	larger boats within 2hrs HW, dinghies at any state of tide
Restrictions:	national inshore speed limit: activity zones may be in force during summer
Facilities:	water point, telephone, toilets, parking for cars and trailers, crane available for cruisers, nearby boatyard: alongside berths sometimes available for cruisers; overnight free, charged thereafter
Charge:	none
Directions:	from D786 heading west from Treguier, take D74 to Port Blanc and follow signs for port where a series of ramps lead from coast road down to beach: longer ramp for larger craft exists near entrance to yachting port
Waters accessed:	Channel

138. Port L'Epine

Type:	concrete slip to hard beach
Suits:	dayboats
Availability:	larger boats towards HW, dinghies at any state of tide
Restrictions:	national inshore speed limit
Facilities:	parking for cars and trailers, telephone, camp site, basic shopping
Charge:	none

Directions:	access is via minor roads from D6 out of Perros-Guirec, D38 and D73 following signs for Port l'Epine past camp site and supermarket
Waters accessed:	Channel

139. Perros-Guirec
Tel: 02 96 23 37 82 (Harbour Master)

Type:	slip to drying outer harbour
Suits:	cruisers
Availability:	within 3hrs HW
Restrictions:	national inshore speed limit: activity zones nearby in summer; whole outer area dries at half tide
Facilities:	parking other side of port may be crowded in summer: toilets, water, telephone. In yacht basin, fuel by arrangement, crane available; chandler nearby, shopping in town centre, small craft fuel from garages. Overnight berth afloat in inner harbour for 7m, FF75
Charge:	none for launching into outer harbour
Directions:	Perros-Guirec is reached by D786/D6 from Treguier or D6 or D788 from Lannion. In town, follow signs for port or beach: launching ramp is immediately outside the barrier enclosing tidal yacht basin
Waters accessed:	Sept Iles and Channel

140. Ploumanach
Tel: 02 96 91 44 31 (Harbour Master)

Type:	slips to inner harbour protected by half-tide barrage
Suits:	cruisers
Availability:	within 3hrs HW for exit from harbour
Restrictions:	speed limit applies in port: half-tide barrier as above
Facilities:	parking may be crowded in summer, telephones, water, toilets, fuel by arrangement, basic shopping in village. Overnight berth for 7m, FF75
Charge:	none for small craft launching in harbour: cruisers may be charged in summer holidays
Directions:	Ploumanach is reached via coastal D788 from Perros-Guirec. In village, follow signs for Le Port. In port, follow road round bay to broad slip suitable for cruisers. another possibly better site exists by tide mill on opposite side of bay: parking here limited but less crowded in summer
Waters accessed:	Sept Iles and Channel

141. Trebeurden
Tel: 02 96 23 64 00 (Harbour Master, Yacht Basin)

Type:	ramps to hard sand beach
Suits:	dinghies
Availability:	best towards HW
Restrictions:	national inshore speed limit: activity zones in force in summer
Facilities:	on sea front, parking, may be crowded in summer, toilets, telephones. In yacht harbour, available on tide: water, electricity, fuel by arrangement, crane available, toilets, showers. Overnight berth for 7m, FF80
Charge:	none for beach launching
Directions:	from Lannion, access via D65: in Trebeurden, follow signs for sea; two usable ramps to the beach exist, one alongside the school, another by the 'Residence la Celtique' flats
Waters accessed:	Lannion Bay

142. Locquemeau

Type:	slip to hard sand in tidal harbour
Suits:	cruisers
Availability:	cruisers on tide, dinghies across sand at any time
Restrictions:	national inshore speed limit: **Caution:** many moorings in summer
Facilities:	parking for cars and trailers, toilets, water, telephones, information point, basic shopping only
Charge:	none
Directions:	from Lannion, take D786 southwest, then D97/88 following signs to Locquemeau: at port, follow quayside round to slip inside breakwater
Waters accessed:	Lannion River and Channel

143. Le Toul an Hery

Type:	ramps to sheltered estuary anchorage
Suits:	dinghies
Availability:	within 2hrs HW
Restrictions:	national inshore speed limit
Facilities:	parking for cars and trailers
Charge:	none
Directions:	from Lannion, take D786 southwest: at Plestin, take D42 for Toul an Hery; coast road leads to stone jetty with ramp alongside, and another to beach facing estuary of River Douron
Waters accessed:	Lannion Bay and Douron Estuary

144. Locquirec

Type:	ramps to beach in drying port
Suits:	dinghies
Availability:	within 3hrs HW approx.
Restrictions:	national inshore speed limit; activity zones may be in force in summer. **Caution:** many moorings in bay
Facilities:	parking for cars and trailers, may be crowded in summer: water, toilets, telephones, inshore lifeboat, basic shopping in village
Charge:	none
Directions:	Locquirec is reached from the D786 via the D42 from Plestin: two ramps to the beach exist in the harbour; another is to be found on the road out of town, signed for Lanmeur, at Moulin de la Rive, possibly the best site
Waters accessed:	Lannion Bay

145. Le Diben
Tel: 02 98 67 30 06 (Mairie - ask for Capitaine du Port)

Type:	ramps to beach or into deep water
Suits:	cruisers
Availability:	all states of tide
Restrictions:	speed limits in port and off beach: fishermen have priority on ramps
Facilities:	water, electricity by arrangement, toilets, telephones, chandler, boatyard, crane available, nearest fuel from garage on main road, lifeboat station
Charge:	none
Directions:	from Lanmeur on D786, take D78 then D46 or D46 from Morlaix to Le Diben village where the road leads to port: ramp to beach for dinghies as you enter village, deep water ramp is at end of harbour mole but may be obstructed by fishing craft and gear
Waters accessed:	Morlaix Bay

146. Terenez
Tel: 02 98 62 28 40 (Harbour Master)

Type:	slip to tidal port
Suits:	cruisers
Availability:	cruisers within 2hrs HW, small craft within 4hrs HW
Restrictions:	speed limit applies in port
Facilities:	parking for cars and trailers, toilets, water, telephone, basic shopping in village
Charge:	none
Directions:	from Morlaix D786, then coastal D76 up Morlaix Bay to Terenez village and follow signs for port: slip gives access to inner harbour
Waters accessed:	Morlaix Bay

147. Le Dourduff

Type:	hard giving access to creek
Suits:	cruisers
Availability:	cruisers on tide, small craft within 2-3hrs HW
Restrictions:	national inshore speed limit: fishermen have priority in parking and launching
Facilities:	limited parking for cars and trailers, telephone
Charge:	none
Directions:	from Morlaix, follow coastal D76 up Morlaix Bay: at Dourduff, turn into village, where road leads to two hards
Waters accessed:	Morlaix Bay

148. Locquenole

Type:	slip by former ferry quay
Suits:	dayboats
Availability:	all states of tide except dead LW
Restrictions:	national inshore speed limit
Facilities:	parking for cars and trailers, telephone and basic shopping in village
Charge:	none
Directions:	from Morlaix, take D73 up west side of Morlaix Estuary: ferry quay is on right, beyond which is a further shingle hard
Waters accessed:	Morlaix Bay

149. Carentec

Type:	ramp to soft beach
Suits:	dinghies
Availability:	within 2hrs HW
Restrictions:	national inshore speed limit: activity zones in force nearby in summer
Facilities:	parking, may be crowded in summer, two chandlers: in town, telephones, general shopping, fuel from local garage, boatyard outside town
Charge:	none
Directions:	from Morlaix take D73 or D58/173. In Carentec ignore signs for Centre Nautique and continue to Le Port and Ile Callot (two chandlers on this road). At Ile Callot are a series of ramps to the beach, and one into rather deeper water at the end of the mole
Waters accessed:	Morlaix Bay

150. Pempoul

Type:	series of ramps to hard beach
Suits:	dayboats
Availability:	within 3hrs HW approx.
Restrictions:	national inshore speed limit: activity zones may be in force in summer. **Note:** sailing club has priority at main slip on race days
Facilities:	parking for cars and trailers, telephones, shopping, fuel in nearby St Pol
Charge:	none
Directions:	Pempoul is a southern adjunct of St Pol de Leon, and access is via minor roads from St Pol. At Centre Nautique there are a series of ramps. **Note:** end of hard is a turning area for trailers and towing vehicles rather than a parking area
Waters accessed:	Morlaix Bay and Channel

151. Roscoff
Tel: 02 98 69 76 37 (Harbour Master)

Type:	slips to drying harbour
Suits:	cruisers
Availability:	cruisers on tide, small craft within 3hrs HW approx.
Restrictions:	speed limit applies in port: care required if navigating in vicinity of ferry terminal at Bloscon
Facilities:	parking for cars and trailers, may be crowded in summer: water, toilets, chandlers, telephone, fuel from local garages. Overnight berth for 7m: old port, FF27, deep water Port Bloscon FF31
Charge:	none
Directions:	in Roscoff town, do not attempt launching at Port Bloscon. In old port, narrow slip at first mole can be difficult; a second slip by chandlery is better. Another slip exists by lighthouse. **Do not use fishing harbour slips**
Waters accessed:	Channel and Ile de Batz

152. Le Dossen

Type:	ramp to hard sand beach
Suits:	dayboats
Availability:	larger craft within 2hrs HW, dinghies at any state of tide
Restrictions:	national inshore speed limit: activity zones may be in force in summer
Facilities:	parking, may be crowded in summer, telephone, toilets, basic shopping
Charge:	none
Directions:	from Roscoff take D769/D58 then turn right onto minor road at St Pol following signs for Dossen: main street leads to port and beach
Waters accessed:	Channel

153. Port de Poulennou

Type:	half-tide ramp
Suits:	dayboats
Availability:	within 3hrs HW approx.
Restrictions:	national inshore speed limit: **Note:** hard must be kept clear for inshore lifeboat
Facilities:	parking for cars and trailers 100m; telephone, basic shopping in village
Charge:	none
Directions:	from D10, follow signs for Bourgorouan, then for Poulennou, where follow signs for Le Port
Waters accessed:	Channel

154. Pors-Meur / Pors-Guen

Type:	half-tide ramps
Suits:	dinghies
Availability:	best within 3hrs HW
Restrictions:	in port, parking reserved for fishermen: speed limit in port and national inshore speed limit; activity zones in force nearby in summer
Facilities:	parking rather limited; nearby telephones, toilets, fuel from garage in Plouescat
Charge:	none
Directions:	from Plouescat village centre follow signs (difficult to spot) via D30 for Pors-Meur and Pors-Guen. At Pors-Meur dinghies can launch down ramp into cove. At Pors-Guen, ramp to beach: restricted fishermen's area is beyond this
Waters accessed:	Channel

155. Brigognan Plage

Type:	ramps to beach
Suits:	dinghies
Availability:	all states of tide
Restrictions:	national inshore speed limit: activity zones in vicinity in summer; **Note:** inshore lifeboat ramp must be kept clear
Facilities:	parking for cars and trailers, crowded in summer
Charge:	none
Directions:	from Lesneven take D125 north, at Goulven turn left onto minor D10, then take D770 following signs for Brigognan Plage. At beach, first ramp is narrow and winding, suitable for trailers but not vehicles: opposite on other side of bay is dinghy ramp to beach. Better ramp is available beside inshore lifeboat station, but must be kept clear at all times
Waters accessed:	Channel

156. Meneham

Type:	concrete causeway
Suits:	dayboats
Availability:	best within 3hrs HW
Restrictions:	national inshore speed limit: fishermen have priority
Facilities:	parking for cars and trailers, mysterious ruins, ghosts by arrangement with druid!
Charge:	none
Directions:	from Lesneven take D125 north, at Goulven turn left onto minor D10, to Kerlouan, then north on minor roads, where signs are minimal, to Meneham : proceed past ruined village to parking area and sea
Waters accessed:	Channel

157. Plage de Vougot

Type:	concret ramp to beach
Suits:	dayboats
Availability:	larger craft towards HW, dinghies at any state of tide
Restrictions:	national inshore speed limit
Facilities:	parking for cars and trailers, may be crowded in summer, telephone on approach road to beach
Charge:	none
Directions:	from Guissent on D10, take minor D52 past Curnic; road leads directly to beach
Waters accessed:	Channel

158. Port de Correjou

Type:	half-tide ramps to sheltered bay
Suits:	cruisers
Availability:	cruisers within 2hrs HW, smaller craft any state of tide except dead LW
Restrictions:	national inshore speed limit: activity zones may be in force in vicinity in summer
Facilities:	parking for cars and trailers, telephone, toilets, inshore lifeboat
Charge:	none
Directions:	from Plougerneau on D10, follow D32 for St Michel, then signs for Port de Correjou: here follow causeway. First ramp suitable for dinghies towards HW, second for all larger craft
Waters accessed:	Channel

159. L'Aberwrac'h
Tel: 02 98 04 91 62 (Harbour Master)

Type:	slips to tidal harbour
Suits:	cruisers
Availability:	cruisers towards HW, small craft within 3hrs HW approx.
Restrictions:	speed limit applies in port: care required owing to intensely busy leisure activity in summer; activity zones in force in vicinity. **Caution:** navigation in this estuary calls for prior study of a local chart for all skippers including those of dinghies
Facilities:	parking for cars and trailers. Fuel: only diesel from pontoon, petrol from garage on main road. Chandler, boatyard. In yacht harbour: toilets, water, telephones. Crane available, lifeboat station. Overnight berth for 7m, from FF67
Charge:	none for launching
Directions:	from Brest, take D788 then D13 north to Lannilis, then follow signs and D128 for L'Aberwrac'h. In town, first ramp is at rear of harbour near discotheque: another exists near port office but is often obstructed by sailing school activities
Waters accessed:	Channel and Atlantic

160. Penn ar Creac'h

Type:	ramp to sheltered inlet
Suits:	dinghies
Availability:	all states of tide except dead LW
Restrictions:	national inshore speed limit: **Caution:** daysailing in this area calls for prior study of a local chart even for dinghy crews
Facilities:	parking for cars and trailers: all other facilities in L'Aberwrac'h
Charge:	none
Directions:	from L'Aberwrac'h, proceed west by minor and badly signed roads to Penn ar Creac'h: a 1:25000 map is helpful on all minor roads in this area
Waters accessed:	Channel and Atlantic

161. St Pabu

Type:	slips by old ferry quay
Suits:	cruisers
Availability:	all states of tide except dead LW
Restrictions:	national inshore speed limit
Facilities:	parking for cars and trailers, toilet, water, telephone, basic supplies in St Pabu village
Charge:	none
Directions:	from Brest take D788 then D13 north, D59/D28 west for Aber Benoit, then follow signs for St Pabu. In village follow signs for Port de Stelac'h, leading to quay with parking area and two slips, one to creek one to beach
Waters accessed:	Aber Benoit Estuary, Channel and Atlantic

162. Portsall

Type:	slips to drying harbour
Suits:	cruisers
Availability:	cruisers towards HW, small craft within 3hrs HW approx.
Restrictions:	speed limit applies in port
Facilities:	ample parking for cars and trailers: water, toilets, chandler, fuel from local garage, lifeboat station, basic shopping in village, overnight mooring free
Charge:	none
Directions:	from Brest follow D26 direct to Portsall. In harbour, slips exist at rear of harbour for dinghies, larger craft by LB station: a better slip is on other side of harbour at Tremazan via minor roads
Waters accessed:	Channel and Atlantic

163. Argenton

Type:	slips to drying harbour
Suits:	dayboats
Availability:	within 2hrs HW
Restrictions:	national inshore speed limit
Facilities:	parking for cars and trailers, telephone and toilets in village
Charge:	none
Directions:	from Portsall, take coastal D27 to Argenton, and continue to Port Argenton: slips exist at head of harbour and by sailing school
Waters accessed:	Channel and Atlantic

164. Port de Porspaul

Type:	slip to drying harbour
Suits:	cruisers
Availability:	cruisers within 1-2hrs HW, smaller craft all states of tide except LW
Restrictions:	national inshore speed limit
Facilities:	parking for cars and trailers, water, toilets, telephone, basic shopping
Charge:	none
Directions:	from Brest take D5 to Lampaule, then south to Plouarzel: at Porspaul, road leads direct to port; slips exist at either end of harbour
Waters accessed:	Channel and Atlantic

165. Plage de Porsliogan

Type:	slip to beach
Suits:	dinghies
Availability:	all states of tide

Restrictions:	national inshore speed limit: activity zones may be in force in vicinity in summer
Facilities:	good parking by nearby monument: all other facilities in nearby Le Conquet
Charge:	none
Directions:	from Brest, take D789 to Le Conquet which, although a port of call for cruisers, is difficult as a launching site: here turn south on coastal D85 to prominent monument; slip nearby
Waters accessed:	Brest Estuary

166. Plage de Porsmilin

Type:	ramp to beach
Suits:	dinghies
Availability:	all states of tide
Restrictions:	national inshore speed limit: activity zones may be in force in summer
Facilities:	parking for cars and trailers, may be crowded in summer, rescue post nearby
Charge:	none
Directions:	from Brest or Le Conquet take D789 direct to Porsmilin, and follow signs for La Plage
Waters accessed:	Brest Estuary

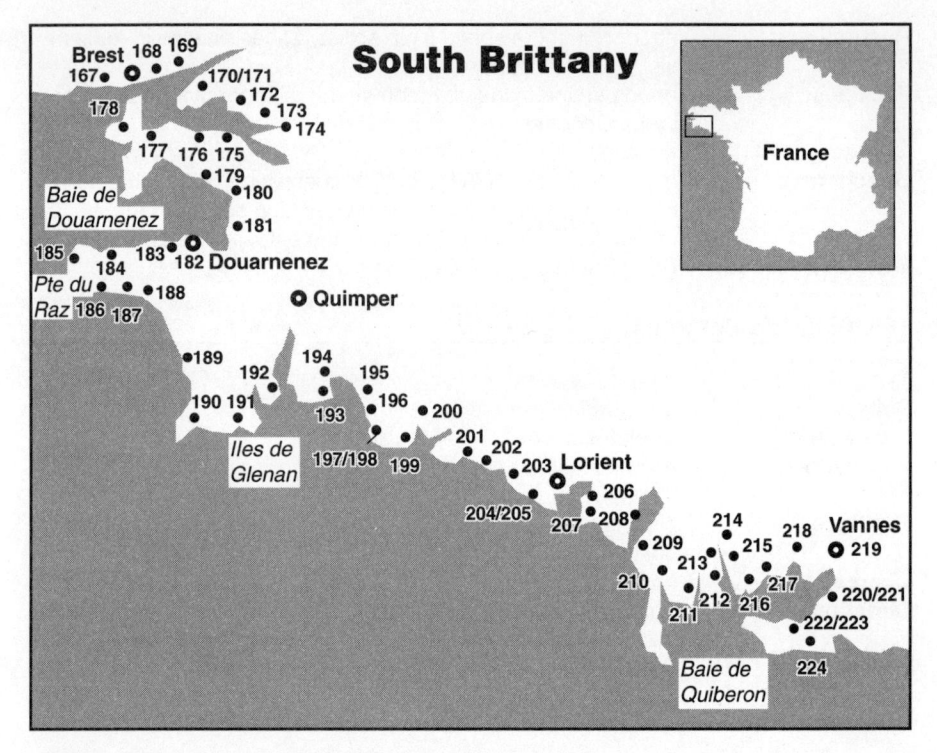

South Brittany

167. Brest - Maison Blanche

Type:	half-tide slip to estaury
Suits:	cruisers
Availability:	within 3hrs HW approx.
Restrictions:	national inshore speed limit: **Caution:** exercise care when navigating Rade de Brest; naval and commercial traffic have priority
Facilities:	limited parking for cars and trailers
Charge:	none
Directions:	Maison Blanche is at the western edge of Brest and is accessed from D789 just outside town by minor roads: consult map; road leads directly to slip
Waters accessed:	Rade de Brest

168. Brest - Moulin Blanc Yacht Harbour
Tel; 02 98 02 20 02 (Marina Harbour Master)

Type:	slip to deep water in yacht harbour
Suits:	cruisers
Availability:	all states of tide
Restrictions:	speed limit applies in port. **Caution:** exercise care when

Facilities:	navigating Rade de Brest; naval and commercial traffic have priority at slip, ample free parking for cars and trailers. In yacht harbour: telephones, toilets, showers, fuel, cranes, electricity. Boatyards and chandlers nearby. Overnight berth for 7m, FF83. In town centre all facilities of major town
Charge:	none for launching
Directions:	Moulin Blanc is to the east of the naval installations of Brest. Follow harbourside road east to Oceanopolis and enter parking area, proceeding to Azenor Cruises office: slip situated behind office
Waters accessed:	Rade de Brest

169. Brest - Port du Passage

Type:	slip to estaury
Suits:	cruisers
Availability:	all states of tide
Restrictions:	speed limit applies in port and estuary
Facilities:	parking for cars and trailers, water point
Charge:	none
Directions:	from Brest town centre, take N165/E60 and follow signs for Le Relecq-Kerhuon: access road to slip is on right
Waters accessed:	River Elorn and Rade de Brest

170. Penn ar Port / Le Caro

Type:	hard leading to estuary
Suits:	cruisers
Availability:	cruisers within 2hrs HW, small craft at all states of tide
Restrictions:	national inshore speed limit
Facilities:	parking for cars and trailers
Charge:	none
Directions:	from Brest, take N165/E60 and D33A to Plougastel Daoulas, then turn onto minor roads to Ste Christine: continue to Le Caro, where road leads to hard
Waters accessed:	Rade de Brest

171. Tinduff

Type:	concrete slip to creek
Suits:	cruisers
Availability:	cruisers within 2hrs HW, small craft at all states of tide
Restrictions:	national inshore speed limit
Facilities:	parking for cars and trailers, toilets, telephone
Charge:	none
Directions:	from N165/E60 at Plougastel Daoulas, follow D33A and minor roads south to Tinduff, where road leads directly to hard
Waters accessed:	Rade de Brest

172. Moulin Mer

Type:	hard giving access to creek
Suits:	dayboats
Availability:	within 3hrs HW
Restrictions:	national inshore speed limit
Facilities:	parking for cars and trailers on roadside, nearby restaurant
Charge:	none
Directions:	continue south from Brest on N165/E60 as far as Daoulas, then take D770, D333 and minor roads, consulting map: signposting to this secluded site is poor
Waters accessed:	Rade de Brest

173. Traon

Type:	half-tide slip to gravel beach
Suits:	dayboats
Availability:	larger craft within 3hrs HW, dinghies at all states of tide
Restrictions:	national inshore speed limit
Facilities:	parking for cars and trailers, telephone in village
Charge:	none
Directions:	follow N165/E60 south to Daoulas then D770 to Hopital Camfrout, from which minor roads lead to Traon: signposting poor, consult map
Waters accessed:	Rade de Brest

174. Le Faou

Type:	draw dock slip to river
Suits:	cruisers
Availability:	cruisers within 2hrs HW
Restrictions:	national inshore speed limit
Facilities:	parking for cars and trailers, basic shopping in town centre
Charge:	none
Directions:	from N165/E60, take minor road for Le Faou Nord. Slips exist on both sides of river bridge for small craft, but better slip is hidden from road at end of long quay on right bank
Waters accessed:	River Faou and Rade de Brest

175. Landevennec

Type:	half-tide ramp to estuary
Suits:	dayboats
Availability:	within 3hrs HW
Restrictions:	national inshore speed limit
Facilities:	parking for cars and trailers, telephone near church, basic shopping in village
Charge:	none

Directions:	from N165 take D791 at Le Faou and D60 or minor roads to Landevennec: steep descent from village centre to Le Port
Waters accessed:	Aulne Estuary and Rade de Brest

176. Le Loc'h

Type:	shingle beach launching
Suits:	dinghies
Availability:	all states of tide
Restrictions:	national inshore speed limit
Facilities:	parking for cars and trailers near beach
Charge:	none
Directions:	from D791 turn right onto D60 and follow signs on minor roads to Le Loc'h: steep descent leads to shingle beach
Waters accessed:	Rade de Brest

177. Le Fret

Type:	ramp to deep water in harbour
Suits:	cruisers
Availability:	all states of tide except dead LW
Restrictions:	speed limit applies in port: nearby Ile Longue is a prohibited Naval area
Facilities:	parking for cars and trailers, water, toilets, telephone, basic shopping in village
Charge:	none
Directions:	Le Fret is reached via the D791 to Crozon and the minor D155. Road leads direct to quayside, where best ramp into deep water is near harbour mole
Waters accessed:	Rade de Brest

178. Camaret
Tel: 02 98 27 95 99 (Marina Harbour Master)

Type:	slip on harbour mole
Suits:	cruisers
Availability:	cruisers within 3hrs HW approx., smaller craft any state of tide
Restrictions:	speed limit applies in port: fishermen have priority on main ramp
Facilities:	parking for cars and trailers, water, toilets, showers, telephones, nearby chandlers, boatyards, crane by arrangement, fuel from nearby garage, all supplies in town centre. Overnight berth for 7m, FF68
Charge:	none for launching
Directions:	Camaret is reached by D791, D887 and D8: in town follow signs for Le Port. In port, several slips to rear of harbour give small craft access but best is on mole within sight of fishermen's chapel
Waters accessed:	Rade de Brest and Atlantic

179. Trez Bellec Plage

Type:	ramps to hard sand beach
Suits:	dinghies
Availability:	all states of tide
Restrictions:	national inshore speed limit: activity zones may be in force in summer
Facilities:	parking for cars and trailers, may be crowded in summer, telephone, nearest supplies in Telgruc
Charge:	none
Directions:	access is via coastal D887 and D208, taking minor road to beach following signs at Telgruc-sur-Mer
Waters accessed:	Douarnenez Bay

180. Rostegoff

Type:	concrete ramp to cove
Suits:	dayboats
Availability:	dayboats within 1-2hrs HW, dinghies at all states of tide
Restrictions:	national inshore speed limit
Facilities:	parking for cars and trailers, telephone at next cove, which has similar access ramp
Charge:	none
Directions:	access is via coastal D887 to Telgruc and then minor roads, and is for experienced drivers!
Waters accessed:	Douarnenez Bay

181. Ty Anquer

Type:	ramp to hard sand beach facing small island
Suits:	dinghies
Availability:	all states of tide
Restrictions:	national inshore speed limit
Facilities:	parking for cars and trailers, telephone, camp site nearby
Charge:	none
Directions:	access from D887 and D47 to Ploeven then minor road to Ty Anquer. **Note:** this road demands alert driving
Waters accessed:	Douarnenez Bay

182. Douarnenez

Note that launching facilities exist on both sides of the Douarnenez complex; those on the west side are signposted as Treboul

Tel: 02 98 92 00 67 (Douarnenez Port- Rhu - old port)
Tel: 02 98 74 02 56 (Treboul Yacht Harbour)

Type:	series of slips to sheltered water
Suits:	cruisers (see below)
Availability:	Douarnenez old port within 3hrs HW approx., Treboul at all states of tide
Restrictions:	speed limits apply inshore and in port: do not enter new fishing port; activity zones in force off beaches
Facilities:	dependent on site: water, telephones, toilets, boatyards, chandlers, marine engineer, fuel from garages and at Treboul. Crane at Treboul. Maritime museum at Port-Rhu. All supplies in town. Overnight berth for 7m, Port-Rhu (traditional boats only) FF30, Treboul FF66
Charge:	none for launching
Directions:	entering by D7 from north, launch sites appear in the following order: (1) old fishing port: slip in front of Capitaine Cook bar. (2) better slip in front of Filets Bleu bar (3) small slip for dinghies into protected water by Port-Rhu breakwater (4) take road round head of creek to Treboul Yacht Harbour: slip to yacht basin by boatyards, sometimes obstructed by boats under repair (5) steeper slip into deep water past Co-operative Maritime (6) slip by Bureau de Port
Waters accessed:	Douarnenez Bay

183. Pors Piron

Type:	beach launching
Suits:	dinghies
Availability:	all states of tide
Restrictions:	national inshore speed limit
Facilities:	parking for cars and trailers, may be crowded in summer, camp site nearby
Charge:	none
Directions:	on coast road to west of Douarnenez: follow signs 7km west of Douarnenez down past camp site to sheltered beach.
Waters accessed:	Douarnenez Bay

184. Pors Lanvers

Type:	beach launching
Suits:	dinghies
Availability:	all states of tide
Restrictions:	national inshore speed limit
Facilities:	limited parking for cars and trailers
Charge:	none

Directions:	access from coastal D7 to west of Douarnenez: follow signs for Pors Lanvers to this wild site
Waters accessed:	Douarnenez Bay

185. Port de Bestree

Type:	natural harbour, portage approach for ultralights
Suits:	ultralights
Availability:	all states of tide
Restrictions:	site essentially for experienced beach canoeists
Facilities:	limited parking on upper access road
Charge:	none
Directions:	via coastal D7 and D784, just south of Pointe du Raz: site has been described as 'pure Boys Own' adventure country
Waters accessed:	Baie d'Audierne

186. Primelin

Type:	ramp to cove harbour
Suits:	dayboats
Availability:	all states of tide but best within 3hrs HW
Restrictions:	national inshore speed limit
Facilities:	parking for cars and trailers, telephone, toilets, water, garage, camp site, basic shopping
Charge:	none
Directions:	access via coastal D784: harbour at edge of village. Slip near former lifeboat station
Waters accessed:	Baie d'Audierne

187. Port Evette
Tel: 02 98 70 02 76 (Mairie - General Enquiries)

Type:	ramp to deep water
Suits:	cruisers
Availability:	within 4hrs HW approx.
Restrictions:	not usable when ferry alongside: speed limit in port and inshore; activity zones nearby
Facilities:	parking for cars and trailers, may be crowded in summer, water, toilets, telephone. Fuel when harbour master present, otherwise from garage in Audierne
Charge:	none in 1997
Directions:	follow D784 to Audierne and then minor coast road south-west to Ste Evette, where launching is extremely difficult but where facilities include repairs and chandlery
Waters accessed:	Baie d'Audierne

188. Pors Poulhan

Type:	cove port with slip
Suits:	dayboats
Availability:	within 3hrs HW approx.
Restrictions:	speed limit applies in port and inshore; surf can be hazardous; fishermen have priority
Facilities:	parking for cars and trailers, telephone, basic shopping
Charge:	none
Directions:	Pors Poulhan is on coast road south-east of Audierne, reached via the D784 and minor roads
Waters accessed:	Baie d'Audierne

189. Penhors

Type:	slip to harbour
Suits:	dayboats
Availability:	best within 3hrs HW
Restrictions:	speed limit applies in harbour and inshore; fishermen have priority; surf may be hazardous;
Facilities:	parking for cars and trailers, telephone, inshore lifeboat
Charge:	none
Directions:	Penhors is reached via the coastal D2, turning onto the D40 at Pouldreuzic
Waters accessed:	Baie d'Audierne

190. St Pierre - Phare d'Eckmuhl

Type:	slip to small natural harbour
Suits:	dayboats
Availability:	within 3hrs HW
Restrictions:	speed limit applies in port and inshore: fishermen have priority; surf outside breakwater may be hazardous;
Facilities:	parking for cars and trailers, basic shopping in village
Charge:	none
Directions:	reached from Penmarc'h, on the D53or D785. Follow signs for St Pierre and Phare d'Eckmuhl. In village, make for lighthouse; two slips nearby
Waters accessed:	Atlantic

191. Lesconil
Tel: 02 98 82 22 97 (Harbour Master)

Type:	slip to head of tidal harbour
Suits:	cruisers
Availability:	cruisers towards HW, smaller craft within 4hrs HW
Restrictions:	speed limits apply in port; fishermen have priority
Facilities:	parking for cars and trailers, toilets, water, telephones, chan-

Charge:	dler, fuel, basic shopping enquire Harbour Master
Directions:	from Pont L'Abbe(off D785) take D102 direct to Lesconil follow signs for port; slip is at landward end of harbour
Waters accessed:	Atlantic

192. Ste Marine
Tel: 02 98 56 38 72 (Harbour Master)

Type:	slip to tidal estuary
Suits:	cruisers
Availability:	within 3hrs HW, but best to launch on flood
Restrictions:	speed limits apply in river and inshore generally
Facilities:	by slip, toilet and water point. Parking for cars and trailers 300m, none available by slip. Nearby yacht harbour has full marina facilities. Basic shopping in town centre, fuel at marina or from local garage
Charge:	none for launching
Directions:	Ste Marine is on the west bank of the Odet or Quimper River and is reached from Quimper via D785 and D44 then minor road before bridge. While it is possible to launch at Benodet, opposite, the available slips are much more difficult for craft larger than dinghies
Waters accessed:	River Odet and Benodet Bay

193. Beg Meil

Type:	half-tide slip to hard sand
Suits:	dinghies
Availability:	all states of tide
Restrictions:	national inshore speed limit: activity zones may be in force in summer
Facilities:	parking for cars and trailers, inshore lifeboat, basic supplies in town centre
Charge:	none
Directions:	access via D45 from Fouesnant: in town follow signs for Le Port; ramp in port, parking just beyond
Waters accessed:	Baie de la Foret

194. La Foret Fouesnant

Type:	slip to hard sand in creek
Suits:	dinghies
Availability:	within 2hrs HW approx.
Restrictions:	speed limits apply in river
Facilities:	parking for cars and trailers, toilets, water point, basic shopping in village
Charge:	none

Directions:	La Foret Fouesnant is on the D44 just east of Fouesnant. In village, follow signs for Vieux Port: two slips from quay give access to creek
Waters accessed:	Baie de la Foret

195. Concarneau
Tel: 02 98 97 57 96 (Harbour Master)

Type:	half-tide slips to drying port
Suits:	cruisers
Availability:	within 3hrs HW approx.
Restrictions:	speed limit in port: fishing craft have right of way and will exercise it determinedly; do not enter fishing port
Facilities:	parking at a distance for cars and trailers. At nearby yacht harbour facilities include toilets, showers, water, electricity, telephones and fuel. All supplies in town centre. Overnight berth for 7m, FF95
Charge:	cruisers will be charged for launching at yacht harbour: old town ramp remains free
Directions:	in Concarneau town, first ramp is near tourist office on Quai Peneroff, near entrance to walled town. Another exists near port office of yacht harbour
Waters accessed:	Baie de la Foret and Atlantic

196. Pointe de Cabellou

Type:	hard launching in sheltered inlet
Suits:	dayboats
Availability:	larger craft within 2hrs HW, dinghies at any state of tide
Restrictions:	national inshore speed limit
Facilities:	parking for cars and trailers, toilet and water point nearby at Anse de Kersos
Charge:	none
Directions:	from Concarneau, follow coast road D783 south and east to signs for Le Cabellou, about 3km
Waters accessed:	Anse de Kersos and Baie de la Foret

197. Raguenes Plage

Type:	ramp to hard sand
Suits:	cruisers
Availability:	cruisers within 1-2hrs HW, smaller craft at any state of tide
Restrictions:	national inshore speed limit
Facilities:	parking for cars and trailers, telephone, nearby camp site
Charge:	none
Directions:	from D783, take D77 west of Pont Aven and follow minor roads to Raguenes Plage; signposting is poor. Ramp is situated near causeway leading to islet
Waters accessed:	Atlantic

198. Anse de Rospico

Type:	cove landing
Suits:	dinghies
Availability:	all states of tide but best within 3hrs HW
Restrictions:	national inshore speed limit
Facilities:	limited parking for cars and trailers
Charge:	none
Directions:	as for Raguenes Plage (site 197) - good map reading skills essential!
Waters accessed:	Atlantic

199. Port Manech

Type:	concrete slip to drying harbour
Suits:	cruisers
Availability:	cruisers within 3hrs HW, small craft at all states of tide except dead LW
Restrictions:	national inshore speed limit: limits also apply in Aven and Belon rivers
Facilities:	parking for cars and trailers, water, toilets
Charge:	none
Directions:	from D783, follow D77 south from west of Pont Aven direct to Port Manech, then follow signs for Le Port
Waters accessed:	Aven and Belon Estuaries

200. Pont Aven

Type:	slips to river at head of navigation
Suits:	cruisers
Availability:	cruisers within 2hrs HW, smaller craft within 3hrs HW approx.
Restrictions:	speed limit applies in river: oyster layings in estuary
Facilities:	parking on quay, water point, electricity theoretically available by arrangement with harbour master when he is present. Shopping in town centre, fuel from garage on edge of town
Charge:	none
Directions:	in Pont Aven town, follow signs for Le Port leading to Quay where there are two draw dock slips
Waters accessed:	Aven and Belon Rivers

201. Port Doelan
Tel; 02 98 71 53 98 (Harbour Master)

Type:	half-tide slips to estuary port
Suits:	cruisers
Availability:	within 3hrs HW
Restrictions:	speed limit applies in river and inshore
Facilities:	parking, may be difficult in summer, water, toilets, telephones,

	nearby boatyard and chandler, inshore lifeboat, fuel from garage on edge of village, basic shopping. Overnight berth for 7m, FF45
Charge:	none for launching
Directions:	take coastal D24 or D16 from Quimperle to Clohars-Carnoet then minor D316. In village, slips are on left bank by lighthouse; another, more sheltered, slip exists in the lower part of the town
Waters accessed:	Atlantic

202. Le Pouldu

Type:	half-tide slip on quay
Suits:	cruisers
Availability:	within 3hrs HW approx.
Restrictions:	speed limit applies in river and inshore
Facilities:	parking for cars and trailers on approach road, telephone, basic shopping in village
Charge:	none
Directions:	from N165/E60 at Quimperle, take D16 to Clohars-Carnoet, then D24 and minor roads to Le Pouldu: quay is at the mouth of River Laita
Waters accessed:	River Laita and Atlantic

203. Le Bas Pouldu

Type:	ramp to half-tide port
Suits:	cruisers
Availability:	cruisers within 2hrs HW, smaller craft at all states of tide except dead LW
Restrictions	speed limit applies in port and inshore: activity zones may be in force in vicinity
Facilities	parking for cars and trailers, telephones, water, toilets at club house by permission
Charge:	none for launching
Directions:	from N165/E60 south-east of Quimperle take D306 to Guidel and Guidel Plage then coastal D152; take port de plaisance access road immediately before large hotel: two slips to hard sand; dinghies may launch over sand nearby at all times
Waters accessed:	Atlantic

204. Kerroch

Type:	ramp to tidal harbour
Suits:	cruisers
Availability:	cruisers towards HW, small craft at all states of tide over sand
Restrictions	speed limit applies in port and inshore
Facilities	parking, toilets, water, telephone and basic shopping in village, garage at Larmor Plage

Charge: none
Directions: from Lorient take D295 and D152 west then minor road: follow signs for Le Port
Waters accessed: Rade de Lorient

205. Lorient - Kernevel Yacht Harbour
Tel: 02 97 65 48 25 (Marina Harbour Master)

Caution: Lorient is an intensely busy naval port with equally congested leisure sailing activity: naval traffic signals in force, obtain local information; naval and commercial craft have right of way

Type: slip into Yacht Harbour
Suits: cruisers
Availability: any state of tide
Restrictions speed limits apply in port: see above caution; obtain local information as to current situation
Facilities parking for cars and trailers. In yacht harbour: water, toilets, showers, telephones. Crane, boatyards, marine engineer, sail-maker nearby. Fuel at yacht club. Overnight berth for 7m, FF90. All other supplies in town
Charge: none for launching
Directions: Kernevel is on west side of Lorient harbour. To find slip, negotiate car park and find outer basin of yacht harbour
Waters accessed: Rade de Lorient

206. Locmicquelic

Type: slips to tidal creek
Suits: cruisers with care
Availability: first slip within 4hrs HW, second slip within 2hrs HW
Restrictions see caution re navigating in Lorient harbour, in previous entry
Facilities parking for cars and trailers, water point, fuel from garage
Charge: none for launching
Directions: from Lorient centre, take D194 then D781 or D781 from N165/E60. In Locmicquelic take harbourside road. First slip by Chantier de la Combe, may occasionally be blocked by yard operations: second slip further on at Port Ste Catherine Yacht Harbour
Waters accessed: Rade de Lorient

207. Riantec

Type: creek launching
Suits: cruisers
Availability: cruisers towards HW, small craft within 2hrs HW
Restrictions speed limit in creek: see caution re navigating in Lorient harbour, in entry 205

Facilities	parking for cars and trailers: all other facilities in Riantec centre
Charge:	none in francs or euros; give spare bread to local ducks
Directions:	from Lorient via D194 and D33 or via D33 from N165/E60. In Riantec, find creek: first site by former tide mill; second is just downstream of road bridge by the church.
Waters accessed:	Rade de Lorient

208. Le Vieux Passage

Type:	ramp in small harbour
Suits:	cruisers
Availability:	cruisers within 1hr HW, small craft within 3hrs HW: half-tide sill below this point
Restrictions	speed limit applies in river: entry and exit regulated in severe weather, obtain local information as to current situation
Facilities	parking for cars and trailers: only other facilities are bar and baker in village
Charge:	none
Directions:	Vieux Passage is just west of bridge over River Etel; from Lorient take D194, D9 then follow signs on minor roads to village and port, which is extremely small and badly signed
Waters accessed:	Etel Estuary

209. Etel
Tel: 02 97 55 46 62 (Harbour Master)

Type:	ramp to creek
Suits:	cruisers
Availability:	all states of tide except LWS
Restrictions	speed limit applies in river: Etel bar is hazardous in severe weather: traffic signals in force. Obtain local information
Facilities	at slip: parking for cars and trailers. In village, basic shopping. Fuel from local garages. In adjoining yacht harbour: water, toilets, crane by arrangement, chandler. Overnight berth for 7m, FF72
Charge:	none for launching
Directions:	Etel is situated on the east bank of the Etel River. Follow signs from D9 and then for Port Etel: two slips from car park into creek; best to investigate on foot
Waters accessed:	Etel River

210. Carnac

Type:	ramp to hard sand
Suits:	dayboats
Availability:	larger craft within 3hrs HW, dinghies at any state of tide
Restrictions	national inshore speed limit: activity zones in force in summer
Facilities	parking, may be crowded in summer: all other supplies in

	Carnac centre
Charge:	none
Directions:	Carnac is on coastal D781: launching site is at Carnac Plage. Past restaurant "Le Plankton"! and yacht club, manoeuvre trailer to opposite mole of small harbour, where there is a broad ramp to hard sand beach
Waters accessed:	Quiberon Bay

211. La Trinite-sur-Mer / St Philibert

Type:	Half-tide ramp to beach
Suits:	cruisers
Availability:	cruisers towards HW, Dinghies at any state of tide
Restrictions:	speed limit applies in river and inshore
Facilities:	at launch site: parking for cars and trailers. In La Trinite, facilities include full marina services in port de plaisanc, overnight berth for 7m, FF90, plus fuel from local garages, numerous boatyards, marine engineer, sailmaker, all supplies
Charge:	none for launching at St Philibert
Directions:	from La Trinite centre, take D781 across river and turn right onto minor D28: ramp is a few hundred metres down this road on right
Waters accessed:	River Crach and Quiberon Bay

212. Le Roch Du

Type:	ramp to Auray river
Suits:	dinghies.
Availability:	within 2hrs HW approx
Restrictions:	national inshore speed limit. **Caution:** Oyster layings nearby
Facilities:	parking for cars and trailers
Charge:	none
Directions:	2km beyond Locmariaquer on D781, minor road is signposted for Le Roch Du: slip near tide mill at head of inlet: little known and unfrequented site
Waters accessed:	Auray River and Morbihan Gulf

213. Fort Espagnol

Type:	narrow slip to Auray River
Suits:	dayboats
Availability:	within 3hrs HW approx
Restrictions:	speed limit applies in river
Facilities:	parking on approach road for cars and trailers. In nearby Crach, garage, basic shopping
Charge:	none
Directions:	from Auray take D28 south to Crach, where take minor turning signed for Fort Espagnol: slip is at end of road; towing vehicles and trailers will have to return up road to find parking space
Waters accessed:	Auray River and Morbihan Gulf

214. Auray (St Goustan)
Tel: 02 97 24 01 23 (Mairie - ask for Harbour Master)

Type:	half-tide slip to Auray River
Suits:	cruisers
Availability:	within 1hr HW approx. **CAUTION:** Beware half-tide sill
Restrictions:	speed limit applies in river
Facilities:	parking for cars and trailers may be crowded, more space available 400m: toilets, shower, telephones, water. Electricity alongside quay by arrangement. Crane available. Chandlery on nearby trading estate. Fuel from garages on edge of town. All supplies from town. Berth alongside: enquire Harbour Master
Charge:	none for launching
Directions:	the port of Auray is St Goustan; in Auray, follow signs for St Goustan. Here make for Quai Benjamin Franklin: small slips exist on upper part of quayside but may be obstructed: larger slip is near port office and loo block
Waters accessed:	Auray River and Morbihan Gulf

215. Le Bono / Mane Verh

Type:	creek launching
Suits:	dayboats
Availability:	within 2hrs HW approx
Restrictions:	national inshore speed limit
Facilities:	on site: parking for cars and trailers. In Le Bono village, telephone, water, toilets, boatyard, garage, shopping. Overnight berths available Le Bono, enquire Mairie (02 97 57 88 98.)
Charge:	none for launching at Mane Verh
Directions:	from Auray, take D101 to Le Bono: 2km beyond Le Bono still on D101 is very minor turning signed for Le Mane Verh; road leads to creek launching site with concrete ramp
Waters accessed:	Bono River and Morbihan Gulf

216. Larmor Baden
Tel: 02 97 57 11 11 (Harbour Master)

Type:	broad full-tide slip
Suits:	cruisers
Availability:	all states of tide
Restrictions:	national inshore speed limit
Facilities:	easy parking for cars and trailers; telephone, water point, toilets, information point, basic shopping in village, garage. Crane available
Charge:	none for unassisted launching
Directions:	from Auray take D101 to Baden, then D316 to Larmor Baden and follow signs for Le Port. Several slips exist, if main slip obstructed small craft may launch from minor slips to beach
Waters accessed:	Morbihan Gulf

217. Port Blanc

Type:	half-tide slip
Suits:	cruisers
Availability:	within 3hrs HW
Restrictions:	national inshore speed limit. **Caution:** quay used by ferry to Ile Aux Moines
Facilities:	parking for cars and trailers, 400m, may be extremely crowded in summer, telephone, toilet
Charge:	FF25 when official present
Directions:	from, Vannes, take D101 south-west, D316 and D316A to Port Blanc: signs for Le Port and Ile Aux Moines lead to slip: vehicles and trailers will need to return to car parks
Waters accessed:	Morbihan Gulf

218. Arradon

Type:	half-tide slip
Suits:	cruisers
Availability:	within 3hrs HW
Restrictions:	national inshore speed limit: site only available when official present
Facilities:	parking for cars and trailers, telephone, water, toilet. Marine engineer nearby. Inshore lifeboat
Charge:	FF25
Directions:	from, Vannes, take D101 and D101A to Arradon, then follow signs for Pointe d'Arradon leading to Basse Nautique. Dinghy sailors note that a further free beach launching site exists beyond Base Nautique via path behind Hotel des Venetes
Waters accessed:	Morbihan Gulf

219. Vannes
Tel: 02 97 54 16 08 (Harbour Master)

Type:	Broad half-tide slip
Suits:	cruisers
Availability:	within 3hrs HW
Restrictions:	national inshore speed limit
Facilities:	at slip: parking for cars and trailers. In Vannes: full marina facilities in yacht harbour behind half-tide lock. Overnight berth for 7m, FF 74. Nearby chandlers, boatyard, sailmaker, garages. All other supplies available in Vannes
Directions:	launch site is not in old port of Vannes but below tidal lock. Follow inner ring road to bridge over port: launch site is just beyond bridge, on Sene side: large parking area gives access to two slips, one of which may be blocked by fishing craft being scrubbed
Waters accessed:	Morbihan Gulf

220. Le Passage

Type:	concrete ramp to sheltered creek
Suits:	dayboats
Availability:	all states of tide
Restrictions:	national inshore speed limit
Facilities:	parking for cars and trailers, may be congested in summer
Charge:	none
Directions:	access from N165/E60 is via D780 to St Armel on Rhuys Peninsula: thence minor road (D198) leads to slip to creek; good map reading essential
Waters accessed:	Morbihan Gulf

221. Ile Tascon

Type:	launch from causeway
Suits:	dayboats
Availability:	within 1-2hrs HW approx
Restrictions:	national inshore speed limit
Facilities:	parking for cars and trailers
Charge:	none
Directions:	access is from N165/E60 and D780: approx. 2km beyond St Armel is minor road signed initially for Lasne, then for the Ile Tascon which leads to causeway leading to island
Waters accessed:	Morbihan Gulf

222. Le Lindin

Type:	creek launching from hard
Suits:	light-draught cruisers
Availability:	within 1-2hrs HW approx
Restrictions:	national inshore speed limit. **Caution** required in Lindin Creek - oyster layings
Facilities:	parking for cars and trailers
Charge:	none
Directions:	Lindin Creek is on the very rural Route du Golfe, running from Sarzeau along the south shore of the Morbihan Gulf: follow coast road to Le Lindin, access to hard is immediately before tide mill
Waters accessed:	Morbihan Gulf

223. Le Logeo

Type:	half-tide ramp to port
Suits:	cruisers
Availability:	cruisers within 3hrs HW, small craft at any time except LWS
Restrictions:	national inshore speed limit. **Caution:** many oyster layings
Facilities:	parking for cars and trailers, may be crowded in summer, water point, toilet. telephone

Charge:	none
Directions:	Le Logeo is reached from the Route du Golfe; beyond Lindin Creek, follow signs for Le Logeo, then for Le Port. Slip descends from quay: if obstructed, small craft may use other ramps to beach on tide
Waters accessed:	Morbihan Gulf

224. Le Tour du Parc

Type:	half-tide slip
Suits:	cruisers
Availability:	cruisers towards HW, small craft within 3hrs HW
Restrictions:	national inshore speed limit: oyster layings: fishermen have priority
Facilities:	limited parking on site for cars and trailers, shellfish for sale. Basic shopping, garage, camp site in village (enquiries Mairie, 02 97 67 30 01, who also have two gites available)
Charge:	none
Directions:	easiest access probably from N165/E60 at Muzillac, via D20 to Surzur, then D195 to Le Tour du Parc, access to waterside in Tour du Parc not obvious, good map essential, but minor road leads to half-tide slip by fishermen's sheds
Waters accessed:	Rade de Penerf

225. Damgan

Type:	beach launching
Suits:	dinghies
Availability:	all states of tide
Restrictions:	national inshore speed limit: activity zones may be in force in summer
Facilities:	on site: parking, may be crowded in summer, toilets. In village: telephone, garage, basic shopping
Charge:	none
Directions:	from Muzillac, take D153. In Damgan follow signs for La Plage: series of ramps on coast road give access to hard sand beach
Waters accessed:	Rade de Penerf

226. Billiers/Penlan

Type:	half-tide slip to creek
Suits:	cruisers
Availability:	cruisers towards HW, smaller craft within 3 hrs HW approx
Restrictions:	national inshore speed limit
Facilities:	parking for cars and trailers, water point, toilet. All other facilities in Billiers - telephones, shopping, garages etc
Charge:	none

Directions:	From Muzillac take D5: the Port of Billiers(!) is in fact Penlan; from town centre, follow signs. Hard and half-tide slip descend from quay. (Marina development has been planned here for some years, but has not yet taken place)
Waters accessed:	Vilaine Estuary and Atlantic

227. Arzal

Type:	foreshore launching
Suits:	dayboats
Availability:	towards HW
Restrictions:	national inshore speed limit: keep clear of tidal barrage
Facilities:	parking for cars and trailers. All other facilities in yacht harbour on opposite bank, include water, electricity, toilets, showers, telephone, chandler, boatyard. Crane available. Overnight berth for 7m, FF70. Tel: 02 99 90 05 86
Charge:	none for foreshore launching
Directions:	from N165/E60 take D139 south. Site is on the tidal barrage, on D139: foreshore accessed immediately after barrage on south side
Waters accessed:	Vilaine Estuary and upper Vilaine River

228. Trehiguier

Type:	half-tide slip to estuary
Suits:	cruisers
Availability:	within 3hrs HW
Restrictions:	national inshore speed limit: fishermen and lifeboat crew have priority
Facilities:	parking for cars and trailers, recently improved: toilets, telephone. Basic supplies in village. Garage at La Roche Bernard
Charge:	none
Directions:	from La Roche Bernard, take D34 via Camoel, then D192 north to Trehiguier: road leads directly to quay
Waters accessed:	Vilaine Estuary

229. Plage de Poudrantais

Type:	ramps to sand and mud beach
Suits:	dinghies
Availability:	best within 3hrs HW
Restrictions:	national inshore speed limit: sailing club have priority at first ramp
Facilities:	parking for cars and trailers, telephone
Charge:	none
Directions:	from La Roche Bernard take D34 to Penestin, follow minor coast road south. Signs lead to Plage du Poudrantais, where first ramp by sailing club leads to sand and mud beach; second

	steeper ramp considered better for vehicles
Waters accessed:	Atlantic

230. Plage de Loscolo

Type:	ramps to hard beach
Suits:	dinghies
Availability:	best within 3hrs HW
Restrictions:	national inshore speed limit
Facilities:	parking for cars and trailers, telephone
Charge:	none
Directions:	as for site 229 but follow minor coast road south beyond Poudrantais. Signposting is poor, good map essential: at beach, concrete ramps lead to hard sand and mud
Waters accessed:	Atlantic

231. Pen Be

Type:	beach launching
Suits:	dinghies
Availability:	Best within 3hrs HW
Restrictions:	national inshore speed limit
Facilities:	parking for cars and trailers; telephone in hamlet
Charge:	none
Directions:	from La Roche Bernard, follow D774 to Herbignac, then D33 to Pont d'Armes. From here to Pen Be promontory via minor roads following map: coast road leads to access to hard beach
Waters accessed:	Atlantic

232. Ile de Rostu

Type:	hard giving access to estuary
Suits:	dinghies
Availability:	within 1-2hrs HW
Restrictions:	national inshore speed limit: nearby oyster layings
Facilities:	parking for cars and trailers: herons; solitude
Charge:	none
Directions:	Wild site best accesssed from La Roche Bernard via D774 and D52 to Mesquer, then following Rue de Rostu, a very minor road leading to large parking area and causeway
Waters accessed:	Pont d'Armes Estuary

233. Kercabellec

Type:	half-tide slip to creek
Suits:	cruisers
Availability:	within 2-3hrs HW

Restrictions:	national inshore speed limit: oyster layings nearby
Facilities:	parking for cars and trailers, telephone. Nearest supplies in Piriac
Charge:	none
Directions:	from La Roche Bernard via D774 and D52 to Mesquer, then follow signs on minor roads leading to tiny harbour with slip
Waters accessed:	Pont d'Armes Estuary and Atlantic

234. Piriac
Tel: 02 40 23 52 32 (Harbour Master)

Type:	slips to drying harbour
Suits:	cruisers
Availability:	cruisers towards HW, small craft from second ramp, within 2-3hrs HW
Restrictions:	Speed limit in port and inshore: whole area dries at half tide
Facilities:	parking for cars and trailers, water, electricity, toilets, showers, telephones, chandler, crane available. Fuel at nearby garages. Overnight berth for 7m, FF64
Charge:	yes, for larger craft launching from main slip - see Harbour Master
Directions:	Piriac is reached via the D52; in town, follow directions for Le Port: main ramp is near port office. Dinghies may launch free on tide from beach at south side of harbour
Waters accessed:	Atlantic

235. La Turballe
Tel: 02 40 23 41 65 (Harbour Master)

Type:	concrete ramp to outside of tidal harbour
Suits:	cruisers
Availability:	all states of tide in fair weather
Restrictions:	national inshore speed limit: speed limit in port. Anchoring prohibited in port approaches; enquire locally
Facilities:	at slip, parking for cars and trailers. In port: full marina facilities include water, electricity, toilets, showers, telephones, fuel. Crane available. Overnight berth, for 7m, FF71. All other supplies in town
Charge:	none for launching
Directions:	from La Baule take D92 north then D774 and D99 west; launching site in La Turballe is far from obvious: on entering town follow signs for port, but do not enter. At south side of harbour is broad slip outside mole giving direct access to sea
Waters accessed:	Atlantic

236. Le Croisic
Tel: 02 40 23 10 95 (Harbour Master)

Type:	slip giving access to creek
Suits:	cruisers
Availability:	cruisers within 1-2 hrs HW, smaller craft within 3hrs HW
Restrictions:	speed limit applies in port: fishermen have priority
Facilities:	at slip, parking for cars and trailers, telephone, toilets in station nearby. Fuel from garages at edge of town. All supplies in town centre. In yacht harbour, water, electricity, telephones, toilets, showers. Chandler nearby. Overnight berth for 7m, FF50
Charge:	none at creek launching
Directions:	from La Baule take N171 to Le Croisic: in town centre, follow signs for SNCF station. A minor road beside station buildings leads to creek, where a concrete ramp gives access for all trailed craft of light draught. All other facilities for visiting boats are in yacht harbour, which is to seaward along the same creek
Waters accessed :	Atlantic

237 Le Pouliguen

Type:	cove launching
Suits:	dinghies
Availability:	all states of tide
Restrictions:	national inshore speed limit
Facilities:	parking for cars and trailers, may be crowded in summer: all other facilities in La Baule
Charge:	none
Directions:	Le Pouliguen lies on the coast road to the west of La Baule, overlooking the town and bay. A series of ramps give access to the beach, the best of which descends to a smaller beach in a rocky cove
Waters accessed:	La Baule Bay and Loire Estuary

238. La Baule
Tel: 02 40 11 97 97 (Harbour Master)

Type:	ramps to beach
Suits:	dinghies
Availability:	any state of tide
Restrictions:	national inshore speed limit: activity zones in force in summer. **Note:** parking in summer is likely to be chaotic
Facilities:	at launching sites, limited parking for cars and trailer; garage at W end of sea front. In yacht harbour to rear of town, launching difficult and not recommended, but water, electricity, fuel, telephones, toilet, showers etc for visiting boats. Overnight berth for 7m, from FF67. All other supplies in town centre

Charge:	none for dinghy launching
Directions:	on La Baule sea front, first ramp on west side of town is opposite Garage de la Plage. No further usable sites until ramps opposite Hotel Manureva(!) Two other ramps at east end of beach.
Waters accessed:	La Baule Bay and Loire Estuary

239. Pornichet
Tel: 02 40 61 61 06 (Yacht Club.)

Type:	ramps to beach
Suits:	dinghies
Availability:	all states of tide
Restrictions:	national inshore speed limit: activity zones in force in vicinity, especially main sea front
Facilities:	at ramps, parking for cars and trailers, may be crowded in summer. At yacht club (tidal port) launching for larger craft by prior arrangement; not free site but toilets, water, telephone available. In adjoining new port, launching only by crane
Charge:	none for dinghy launching from beach
Directions:	all facilities accessed from Pornichet sea front. One ramp available at west end of front; beyond this no public access except yacht club by prior arrangement until east end of front, where turn onto coastal D292. Bonne Source, at edge of town, has series of broad ramps to beach, accessible to trailers and 4 x 4 vehicles
Waters accessed:	Loire Estuary

240. Ste Marguerite

Type:	beach launching
Suits:	dinghies
Availability:	all states of tide
Restrictions:	national inshore speed limit: activity zones in force in vicinity in summer
Facilities:	parking for cars and trailer, may be crowded in summer. Nearby garage, telephone, basic shopping
Charge:	none
Directions:	from La Baule follow D92 to Pornichet then coastal D292 to Ste Marguerite, there are a series of access points to beach: first at traffic lights, second at Plage des Jaunais where signpost indicates boat launching area. Further site exists to the east at Parc de l'Eve, with better parking and broad access to beach
Waters accessed:	Loire Estuary

241. St Nazaire

Type:	ramps to beach
Suits:	dinghies
Availability:	all states of tide
Restrictions:	national inshore speed limit: activity zones may be in force in summer. **Caution:** special care required in vicinity of commercial port entrance; use by leisure craft discouraged, no overnight berths available except in emergency
Facilities:	parking for cars and trailers, garages, toilets at west end of sea front, inshore lifeboat. All supplies in town, chandler near commercial port
Charge:	none
Directions:	all facilities accessed from sea front road. First slip entering from west used by lifeboat and must be cleared after use. Two more usable slips by war memorial. At east end, near pilot station, soft sand beach suitable for launching lighter dinghies
Waters accessed:	Loire Estuary

242. Port du Brivet

Type:	creek port
Suits:	cruisers provided lowering mast
Availability:	within 1-2 hrs HW
Restrictions:	speed limit in port and creek: fixed bridge gives 2m clearance at HWS
Facilities:	easy parking for cars and trailers, toilet, water tap, cafe, telephone. Garage and basic shopping nearby
Charge:	none
Directions:	easiest access is from St Nazaire centre or main D213 near St Nazaire Bridge. Follow minor roads and generally poor signs for suburban Port du Brivet, close by the west side of the estuary bridge: two slips, one narrow, one broad. Take care, soft mud beyond slip
Waters accessed:	Loire Estuary.

243. Lavau-sur-Loire

Type:	creek port off Loire Estuary
Suits:	dayboats
Availability:	within 1-2hrs HW
Restrictions:	narrow access channel: speed limit applies
Facilities:	parking for cars and trailers, telephone, cafe
Charge:	none
Directions:	from St Nazaire take N171 east and follow signs for Savenay: there follow minor D3 to Lavau village where minor streets lead to small basin by sluice and Cafe du Port: two slips nearby
Waters accessed:	Loire Estuary

244. Ste Anne

Type:	creek port off Loire Estuary
Suits:	dayboats
Availability:	within 1-2hrs HW
Restrictions:	narrow creek though wider than Lavau: speed limit applies: gate must be closed against wandering livestock on marshes
Facilities:	easy parking for cars and trailers
Charge:	none
Directions:	from Savenay D17 then minor D93 to Bouee and follow minor roads to Ste Anne. Creek basin is wild site; approach gate keeps livestock off road
Waters accessed:	Loire Estuary

245. Basse-Indre

Type:	slips to Loire tideway
Suits:	cruisers
Availability:	within 3hrs HW approx
Restrictions:	national inshore speed limit; exercise care among moorings; commercial traffic has priority
Facilities:	parking for cars and trailers near ferry, 200m; telephones, toilets, nearby; garage. All supplies in Basse-Indre or Nantes
Charge:	none
Directions:	Basse-Indre is a western suburb of Nantes, reached via D75; launching site is 200m upstream of ferry. Two broad slips give direct access to tideway; some experience of similar tidal waters desirable
Waters accessed:	Loire tideway

246. Trentemoult
Tel: 02 40 84 09 14 (Harbour Master)

Type:	slip to rear of drying port
Suits:	light draught cruisers
Availability:	HW only
Restrictions:	speed limit applies inshore: exercise care navigating tideway, commercial craft have priority. **Note:** Trentemoult is usually severely silted
Facilities:	easy parking for cars and trailers, toilets, shower, telephone, water, electricity by arrangement. Overnight berth free (24 hours mooring) Garage nearby; chandlers and all other supplies in Nantes
Charge:	none
Directions:	Trentemoult is a southern suburb of Nantes, reached via Reze (Nantes south,) following signs on minor roads - note that most road maps are misleading: port is on main riverside road, Quai Surcouf
Waters accesssed:	Loire Tideway

South Brittany and the Western Rivers

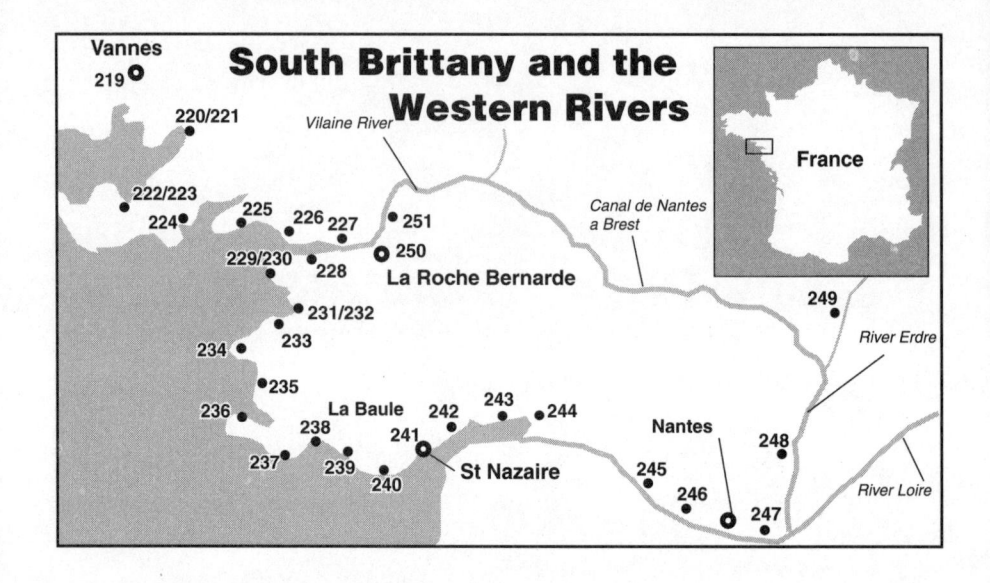

The navigable rivers and inland waterways of Western France offer a fascinating and largely unspoilt cruising ground for small craft. While the Erdre, Breton Canals, tidal Loire to Angers and the navigable Mayenne are workable cruising grounds for all trailed cruisers with the exception of fin keel yachts on the tidal Loire, the upper Loire and Vienne, although offering wide expanses of water, must be regarded as small craft country. On the upper Loire, the navigable channel for motor and sailing craft is usually narrow and tortuous, and shifts from season to season. It is normally buoyed or marked by withies in the more difficult sections. Rowing craft and canoes can and do navigate outside the channel, but must expect grounding from time to time. Care should be taken in shoving off from the banks, as the Loire's sandy bed is extremely soft in places, and the channels may be steep-to; it is usually better to refloat using oars or paddles. Note that the upper Loire cannot be entered direct from the lower river owing to obstructions at the Ponts de Ce in Angers. Plans have been mooted for many years for a lock or boat slide, but no progress seems to have been made on the ground to date.

British visitors will be delighted to discover that the Reseau de l'Ouest, as the Western rivers are usually called, remain a free navigation zone, where no licences or tolls exist, and none are envisaged for the foreseeable future.

South Brittany and the Western Rivers

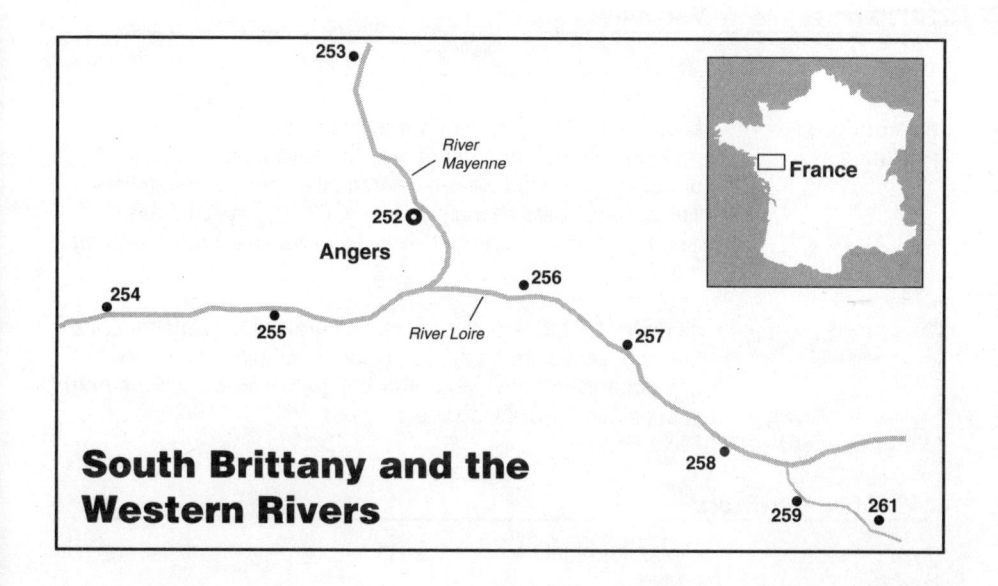

Only on the lower Loire, which is administered by Voies Navigables de France, the inland waterways administration, is a licence necessary for craft over 5m in length and 6hp, and this is collected in the form of a toll payable when passing through the lock at Angers linking the Loire with the Mayenne.

The Breton Canals are best accessed by trailed craft at Lyvet le Port in the north, (see page 53), the Erdre navigation in the south, or on the River Vilaine. It is also possible for small craft to enter the semi-closed Western section from the Rade de Brest, but it should be noted that at the time of writing repairs are not complete following the disastrous floods of a few years ago, and that portages may still prove necessary at the upper locks. The best access to the Mayenne remains at Angers, although improvement works are planned at a number of riverside towns to enable cruisers to launch easily. On the upper Loire, virtually every riverside town has one or more launching sites for small trailed craft, although the standard of maintenance and the navigability of the quayside water can vary dramatically. We have listed some of the best Loire sites, but it should be borne in mind that this list is not exhaustive, and that a little exploration is usually more than worthwhile.

RIVER ERDRE

247. Nantes, Ile de Versailles

Type:	slip to non-tidal river
Suits:	cruisers
Restrictions:	speed limit in port: lowering mast essential
Facilities:	parking for cars and trailers may be difficult near river; in doubt ask port staff. On Ile de Versailles, fuel, water, toilets. Telephone, basic shopping nearby. Chandlery Quai des Antilles - ask port staff. All supplies in Nantes. Free overnight mooring
Charge:	none
Directions:	Ile de Versailles is in Nantes city centre, follow signs for Gare Fluviale: access to Ile de Versailles is via minor roads, semi-pedestrianised area: just below bridge to island and 50m from yacht station is draw dock slip
Waters accessed:	River Erdre

248. Suce-sur-Erdre

Type:	slip to non-tidal river
Suits:	cruisers
Restrictions:	speed limit on upper Erdre: lowering mast essential
Facilities:	parking currently being expanded, toilets, telephone. water, garage nearby; basic shopping in Suce. Boatyard nearby, chandler, information office. Free overnight mooring
Charge:	none
Directions:	Suce is reached from Nantes via D69 north; port is in lower part of town centre, with slip upstream of bridge near tourist office. Entrance to Canal de Nantes a Brest approx. 7km upstream
Waters accessed:	River Erdre

249. Nort-sur-Erdre

Type:	narrow slip to non-tidal river
Suits:	small craft
Restrictions:	speed limit in river; lowering mast essential
Facilities:	easy parking for cars and trailers, telephone, toilets, garage nearby. Free overnight mooring. Basic shopping in Nort
Charge:	none
Directions:	Nort is most easily reached from Nantes via the D69 to Suce and D26 to Nort. In town centre, follow signs for Base Nautique by main bridge. Nort is 6m above entrance to Canal de Nantes a Brest
Waters accessed:	River Erdre

RIVER VILAINE

250. La Roche Bernard

Type:	slips to non-tidal river
Suits:	dayboats/small cruisers: larger trailed cruisers may launch by crane at adjoining boatyards by arrangement
Restrictions:	town slips in busy tourist area, best used during morning, ideally before 10am
Facilities:	at slip, car park, 200m (no trailers). At neighbouring boatyard and yacht basin, toilets, showers, telephone, water, fuel alongside or from garage in town. Crane available. All supplies in La Roche Bernard
Charge:	none for launching at slip
Directions:	La Roche Bernard is on main N165/E60. Follow signs for town centre and then for port. Slip is on old town quay with bars and restaurants opposite hence need for early morning use in holiday season
Waters accessed:	River Vilaine and Breton canals

251. Trevineuc

Type:	slip to non-tidal river
Suits:	cruisers
Facilities:	easy parking for cars and trailers, telephone, water, toilet, nearby boatyard
Charge:	none for launching
Directions:	Trevineuc, a far better site for cruiser launching than La Roche Bernard, is reached by minor roads from La Roche Bernard following signs initially for Nivillac, then for Trevineuc. Signposting is poor and a good map essential. When found, road leads to a hard public slip, with the boatyard's railway slip alongside
Waters accessed:	River Vilaine and Breton canals.

RIVER MAYENNE

252. Angers

Type:	slip to non-tidal river
Suits:	cruisers
Restrictions:	lowering mast essential
Facilities:	near slip, toilets, telephone, water. Parking may be difficult, larger parking area upstream near old university buildings. Fuel from local garages. All supplies in Angers town centre. Crane available, by arrangement, upstream at nearby yacht club
Charge:	none
Directions:	site is in town centre on west bank of River Maine (which becomes the Mayenne upstream of Angers.) At main town bridge, the furthest downstream in town centre, turn left to small craft basin
Waters accessed:	Rivers Maine, Mayenne, Sarthe and tidal Loire (toll payable at lock)

253. Chateau-Gontier

Type:	slip to non-tidal river
Suits:	cruisers
Restrictions:	lowering mast essential
Facilities:	parking for cars and trailers, telephones. Fuel from nearby garages. Most supplies in town centre
Charge:	none
Directions:	this less industrial access point to the Mayenne is best reached from Angers via N162. Site is in town centre within site of main bridge, on old quay
Waters accessed:	River Mayenne

TIDAL LOIRE

The Loire is navigable by craft entering from the sea as far as its junction with the River Maine at Bouchemaine lock, Angers. It should be noted that the channel can silt at certain seasons, and that buoyage should be strictly heeded. Larger craft navigating this section of the Loire are recommended to have available a cruising guide such as the Guide des Canaux Bretons et de la Loire, available from chandlers or the Erdre Port Office in Nantes. Sailing craft should regard a lowering mast as essential

254. Ancenis

Type:	ramp to tidal Loire
Suits:	dayboats
Availability:	not at LWS
Restrictions:	lowering mast required

Facilities:	parking for cars and trailers, fuel from garage in town, telephones, basic supplies in town centre
Charge:	none
Directions:	Ancenis is inland from Nantes on N23: follow signs for town centre. Old small craft landing is on right bank just upstream of bridge carrying D763
Waters accessed:	Lower Loire

255. Montjean-sur-Loire

Type:	ramp to tidal Loire
Suits:	cruisers
Availability:	all states of tide
Restrictions:	lowering mast required
Facilities:	telephone, toilets, parking for cars and trailers, basic shopping in town centre, fuel from nearby garages
Charge:	none
Directions:	situated on the left or south bank, Montjean is most easily reached from Nantes via the N23, turning south onto D15 at Champtoce-sur-Loire and crossing the river: town quay with stone slip is within sight of the bridge
Waters accessed:	Lower Loire

UPPER LOIRE

Classed as a "Wild River," the upper Loire and its tributary the Vienne are still regularly navigated by small craft and the traditional flat-bottomed barges of the region as far as Tours and Chinon. Lack of water is a problem for larger craft, especially those with outboards and Z drives, during dry summers in some reaches; for these craft the Loire is usually best explored in spring and early summer. Small craft can navigate without difficulty at all times, but motor craft in particular should pay close attention to navigation marks in the buoyed sections, as the channel is often narrow and tortuous. Several wider and deeper sections exist such as the Saumur reach, where dinghy sailing takes place on a regular basis. Dinghies and catamarans with taller masts should however be aware of bridge clearances, and be prepared to lower masts where necessary. All the riverside towns have old quays of varying quality, and camp sites abound either on the riverside or within a short distance. Fresh water is a problem for cruising boats, and a supply should be obtained at a camp site or garage if overnight wild camping aboard or on one of the many uninhabited islands is envisaged. Landing on these is normally permitted unless signs forbid mooring and camping as on some of the larger islands where farms still exist. The Loire traditional sail fraternity are always ready to give advice to visitors exploring the river with small craft, and dinghy cruisers, canoeists and others with at least a little French are assured a warm welcome. It should be borne in mind on the other hand that PWCs and similar craft are officially and unofficially discouraged, and that water-ski activities are illegal except in a few defined areas where a club exists.

256. La Bohalle

Type:	slip by town quay
Suits:	small craft
Facilities:	parking for cars and trailers, toilets, telephone at Mairie (near church), basic shopping. Garages in Angers. Wild camping on island opposite
Charge:	none
Directions:	situated on the right bank, La Bohalle is reached from Angers via the riverside D952. In village centre, turn down onto town quay
Charge:	none
Waters accessed:	Upper Loire

257. Les Rosiers-sur-Loire (Gennes)

Type:	slip into deep water
Suits:	dayboats and small cruisers
Facilities:	parking for cars and trailers, two camp sites nearby. Most shopping in town. Garages
Charge:	none
Directions:	from Angers, follow D952 to Les Rosiers and cross bridge. The best launching site is on the left or south bank, technically Gennes, and just downstream of the bridge
Charge:	none
Waters accessed:	Upper Loire

258. Saumur

Type:	slips from town quay to river: also slip at sailing club
Suits:	dayboats and small cruisers
Facilities:	parking for cars and trailers at slips. In town, telephones, toilets near tourist information office. Fuel from nearby garages. Camp site opposite and upstream. All supplies in town. Chandler 3km S of town on D960
Charge:	none
Directions:	site visible near town centre, on left or south bank and downstream of town centre bridge, near tourist information office. Turn off road into riverside parking area. Two slips, at upstream and downstream ends of parking area. Two more slips exist on same bank ustream of bridge but are somewhat less accessible. Best slip for cruisers is opposite on right bank at sailing club: ask permission when anyone present
Charge:	none
Waters accessed:	Upper Loire

259. Montsoreau

Type:	slip from town quay
Suits:	small cruisers
Facilities:	parking for cars and trailers, toilets, water, telephones, camp site nearby. Garage and basic supplies in town. Water ski area (1997, check current situation on arrival)
Charge:	none
Directions:	from Saumur, follow riverside D947 along south bank to Montsoreau; access to quay from road
Waters accessed:	Upper Loire and River Vienne

260. Chouze-sur-Loire

Type:	slip from quay
Suits:	small craft
Facilities:	limited parking for cars ad trailers, telephones, toilets near Mairie, garage, basic shopping
Charge:	none
Directions:	from Saumur take N152/E60 toChouze on the north bank of the Loire; quay is off main road in village centre: access to rear of Mairie
Waters accessed:	Rivers Loire and Vienne

261. Chinon

Type:	(1) slip from quay (2) beach in riverside games area
Suits:	small craft
Facilities:	parking for cars and trailers, telephones and all supplies in town centre. Garage nearby. Camp site on south bank
Charge:	none
Directions:	Chinon is reached via D751 from Tours or Saumur. Both sites are in town centre; first is on quay upstream of bridge, on right or north bank. Second is on opposite bank, downstream of bridge; access via riverside games area for light craft
Waters accessed:	Rivers Vienne and Loire

Glossary
English - French

Alongside (come alongside) - accoster
Anchor - *n* ancre, f. *v* jeter l'ancre, mouiller
Awash - á fleur d'eau
Axle - essieu, m
Bail - *v* écoper
Bailer - écope, f
Bank - rive, f
Basin - bassin, m
Batten (sail) - latte, f
Bay - baie, anse, f
Beacon - balise, f
Beam (width) - maitre bau, largeur, f
Beam (deck beam) - barrot, m
Bearing (engine) - roulement, m
Bearing (compass) - relèvement, m
Belay - *v* amarrer
Block - poulie, f
Boathook - gaffe, f
Bollard - poupée, bitte, f
Bottom - fond, m
Bow - avant, m
Bowline (hitch) - noeud de chaise, f: (of lug or squaresail) bouline, f
Bowsprit - beaupré, bout-dehors, m
Bucket - seau, m
Bulbs (lighting) - ampoules, f
Bulkhead - cloison, f
Bung - nable, f
Buoy - bouée, f
Buoyancy - flottabilité, f
Capsize - *n* chavirage, f. *v* chavirer
Carvel (built) - à bordée classique, à franc-bord
Caulking - calfatage
Centreboard - dérive
Centreboard case - puits de dérive
Cleat - *n* taquet
Clinker (built) - à clins
Clinker (strake) - clin, m
Coachroof - rouf, m
Coaming - hiloire, f
Compass - boussole, f: compas, m
  Bearing Compass - compas de relèvement, m
Contact breaker (engine) - contact de rupture, interrupteur, m
Countersink - *v* fraiser

Cove - anse, f: pors, port, m
Cover - taud, m
Cringle - patte, f
Depth - profondeur, f
Deviation - déviation, f
Diesel (fuel) - gas-oil, m: (engine) diesel, m
Dinghy (sailing) - dériveur, m: (pram) annexe, f
Dive - *v* plonger
Diver - plongeur
Downstream - en aval
Draught - tirant d'eau; (air draught) tirant d'air, m
Ease sheets - choquer
Ebb - jusant, m; marée jusant, f
Echo sounder - sondeur, m
Eddy - remous, m
Eyelet - oellet
Fairlead - chaumard, m
Ferry - ferry, bac, m
Fit out - *v* armer
Flare - feu de détresse, m; fusée, pyrotechnique, f
Flood (tide) - marée montant
Floor (construction) - varangue
Frame - membrure
Freeboard - franc-bord
Gaff (rig) - gréement à corne, m
Garboard - galbord, m
Gauge (engine) - jauge, f
Glue - colle, f (colle-epoxy, -resorcinol, etc.)
GRP - polyester, m; **resin** - resine, f; **cloth** - mat-tissu, m; **hardener** - catalyste, f
Gudgeon - aiguillot, m
Gunwale - liston, m
Halyard - drisse, f
Haul - *v* hisser
Heel (of boat) - gîte, f; (of keel) talon de quille, m
Hitch/unhitch - *v* accrocher/décrocher
Hoist - *v* hisser
Ignition (engine) - allumage, m
Inflatable (dinghy) - pneumatique, f
Insulating tape - scotch, m
Insulation - isolation, f
Jack - cric, m
Jetty - jetée, f

111

Jib - foc, m
Jury rig - gréement de fortune, m
Keel - quille, f
Keelson/hog - carlingue, m
Knee (construction) - courbe, f
Knot - nœud, m
Larch - mélèze, m
Lead - plomb, m
Leadline - sonde, f
Leak - *n* fuite, f; *v* faire de l'eau
Lee - sous le vente, m
Leeboard - dérive laterale, f
Let go (mooring) - *v* lâcher
Lifejacket - gilet de sauvetage, m
Lock/sluice - écluse, f
Log (speed) - loch, m; (book) livre de bord, m
Lower (sail) - *v* amener
Lugsail - voile à tiers, f
Mainsail - grand'voile, f
Mahogany - acajou, m
Mizzen - artimon, m
Mooring - mouillage, corps-mort, m
Mussel stake - bouchot, m
Nail - pointe, f; carvel, m
Nautical almanac - almanach, m
Navigation - navigation, f
Navigation light - feu de route, m
Number plate - plaque d'immatriculation, f
Oak - chêne, m
Oar - aviron, m; rame, f
Oilskins - cirés, f
Outboard (motor)- hors-bord, m
Padlock - cadenas, m
Paint - peinture, f; (antifouling) fouling
Pennant/burgee - guidon, m
Pin (rigging) - goupille, f
Pine (wood) - sapin, Douglas, m
Pintle - fémelot, m
Pitch (tar) - goudron, m
Pitch-pine - pitchpin, m
Plug (engine) - bougie, f
Plywood - contre-plaqué; marine ply - contreplaqué marine, m
Propeller - hélice, f
Pulpit - balcon avant, m; pushpit balcon arrière, m
Pump - pompe, f; **bilge-pump** - pompe de cale
Rear lights - feu d'arrière, m
Reef - *n* ris, m; bande de ris, f: *v* arriser
Rope - cordage, m; corde, f: mooring rope - aussière, f
Row - *v* ramer
Rowlock - dame de nage, f; tolet, m
Rudder - gouvernail, safran, m
Scarph (construction) - écart, m
Screw - vis, f
Scull - *v* godiller
Sculling oar - godille
Self-bailer - autovideur, m
Shackle - manille, f
Shaft (propeller) - arbre (d'helice), m
Sheer - tonture, f
Sheet (rigging) - écoute, f
Shoal - bas-fond, m
Slip - cale,f
Spar - espar, m
Spare wheel - roue de secours, f
Splice - *n* épissure, f
Stanchion - chandelier, m
Start (engine) - *v* démarrer
Starter - démarreur, m
Stay - étai, m
Stem - étrave, f
Sternpost - étambot, m
Survey - expertise, f
Surveyor - expert maritime, m
Tack (of sail) - point d'amure, m; *v* virer de bord
Tackle - palan, m
Tar - goudron, coltar, m
Tarpaulin - bâche, f
Tender/ dinghy - annexe, f
Tiller - barre, f
Tow - *v* remorquer
Towbar - barre d'attelage, f
Trailer - remorque, f **break back trailer** - remorque basculante/articulée
Transom - tableau, m
Trawler - chalutier, m
Tug - remorqueur, m
Tyre - pneu, m
Upstream - en amont
Variation (compass) - variation, f
Warp - amarre, aussière, f
Weather forecast - météo, f
Weld - *n* soudure, f; *v* souder
Winch (sheet/halyard) - winch; (anchor) guindeau; (trailer/vehicle) treuil, m
Wire - fil, m

Index

Agon-Coutainville	45	Concarneau	83
Ambleteuse	19	Courseulles-sur-Mer	37
Ancenis	106	Damgan	92
Angers	106	Deauville	34
Anse de Rospico	84	Dielette	43
Argenton	72	Dieppe	30
Arradon	90	Dinard, Clair de la Lune	54
Arromanches	38	Dives-sur-Mer	35
Arzal	93	Douarnenez	79
Audresselles	19	Dunes de Mont St Frieux	21
Ault	26	Dunkirk / Dunkerque	16
Auray	89	Equihen Plage	21
Barfleur	41	Erdre River	104
Basse-Indre	99	Erquy	57
Beg Meil	82	Etaples	22
Benodet	82	Etel	87
Berck Plage	24	Fecamp	33
Bernieres-sur-Mer	37	Fort Espagnol	88
Billiers	92	Franceville	36
Binic	58	Gatteville	41
Blonville	34	Gennes	108
Boulogne	20	Goury	43
Bray-Dunes	15	Grandcamp-Maisy	39
Brehec	59	Granville	45
Brest - Maison Blanche	74	Gravelines	16
Brest - Moulin Blanc Yacht Harbour	74	Greve de Port Briac	51
Brest - Port du Passage	75	Greve St Marc	59
Brigognan Plage	69	Groffliers	24
Cabourg	35	Haire-de-la-Vanlee	45
Calais	17	Hardelot Plage	21
Camaret	77	Havre de Rotheneuf	51
Cancale	50	Havre-Antifer	33
Cap Blanc Nez	18	Hermanville	36
Cap Gris Nez	19	Hirel	50
Cap Hornu	25	Ile de Rostu	94
Carentec	67	Ile Tascon	91
Carnac	87	Isigny	39
Carteret	44	Kercabellec	94
Cayeux	25	Kernevel	86
Chateau-Gontier	106	Kerroch	85
Cherbourg	42	L'Aberwrac'h	71
Cherrueix	48	La Baule	96
Chinon	109	La Bohalle	108
Chouze-sur-Loire	109	La Foret Fouesnant	82
Coleville	36	La Hogue	42

La Hoguette	42
La Jouvente	53
La Riviere	43
La Roche Bernard	105
La Roche Jaune	62
La Trinite-sur-Mer	88
La Turballe	95
Landemer	41
Landevennec	76
Larmor	61
Larmor Baden	89
Lavau-sur-Loire	99
Le Bas Pouldu	85
Le Bequet	42
Le Bono	89
Le Caro	75
Le Conquet	73
Le Croisic	96
Le Crotoy	24
Le Diben	66
Le Dossen	68
Le Dourduff	67
Le Faou	76
Le Fret	77
Le Grand Porcan	50
Le Grand Vey	40
Le Havre	34
Le Hourdel	25
Le Lindin	91
Le Lion-sur-Mer	37
Le Loc'h	77
Le Logeo	91
Le Passage	91
Le Portel	20
Le Pouldu	85
Le Pouliguen	96
Le Rieul	55
Le Roch Du	88
Le Toul an Hery	65
Le Touquet	22
Le Tour du Parc	92
Le Vieux Passage	87
Le Vivier-sur-Mer	49
Leffrinckoucke	15
Les Hemmes	17
Les Rosiers-sur-Loire	108
Lesconil	81
Lezardrieux	61
Locmicquelic	86
Locquemeau	65
Locquenole	67
Locquirec	66
Loguivy-sur-Mer	61
Loire River (tidal)	106
Loire River (upper)	107
Lorient	86
Lyvet le Port	53
Malo-les-Bains	16
Mane Verh	89
Mayenne River	106
Meneham	70
Merlimont Plage	23
Merville	35
Mesnil-Val	30
Mont St. Michel	46
Montjean-sur-Loire	107
Montsoreau	109
Mordreuc	53
Moulin Mer	76
Nantes	104
Nort-sur-Erdre	104
Notre Dame du Guildo	55
Omaha Beach	38
Omonville-La-Rogue	43
Ouistreham	36
Paimpol	60
Paris Plage	23
Pempoul	68
Pen Be	94
Penhors	81
Penlan	92
Penn ar Creac'h	71
Penn ar Port	75
Perros-Guirec	64
Petites Dalles, Grandes Dalles	32
Piriac	95
Plage de Loscolo	94
Plage de Palus	59
Plage de Porsliogan	72
Plage de Porsmilin	73
Plage de Poudrantais	93
Plage de Vougot	70
Plage du Roue	53
Pleheral Plage	56
Ploumanach	64
Pointe de Cabellou	83

Location	Page	Location	Page
Pointe du Champ du Port	57	Sciotot	44
Pont Aven	84	St Aubin-sur-Mer	31
Pornichet	97	St Briac-sur-Mer	55
Pors Even	60	St Brieuc	58
Pors Lanvers	79	St Cast le Guildo	56
Pors Piron	79	St Gabriel Plage	22
Pors Poulhan	81	St Goustan	89
Pors Scaff	63	St Jacut de la Mer	55
Pors-Guen	69	St Malo	52
Pors-Meur	69	St Nazaire	98
Port Beni	62	St Pabu	71
Port Blanc, Brittany	63	St Philibert	88
Port Blanc, Morbihan	90	St Pierre	81
Port de Bestree	80	St Pierre-en-Port	32
Port de Correjou	70	St Quay Portrieux	58
Port de la Chaine	62	St Suliac	52
Port de Legue	58	St Vaast-la-Hougue	40
Port de Porspaul	72	St Valery-en-Caux	32
Port de Poulennou	69	St Valery-sur-Somme	25
Port Doelan	84	Ste Anne	99
Port du Brivet	98	Ste Cecilie Plage	21
Port Evette	80	Ste Marine	82
Port Jaquet	56	Ste Marguerite, Normandy	31
Port l'Ailly	31	Ste Marguerite, South Brittany	97
Port L'Epine	63	Stella Plage	23
Port La Richardais	54	Suce-sur-Erdre	104
Port Lazo	60	Terenez	66
Port Manech	84	Tinduff	75
Port Mer	51	Traon	76
Port Nieux	56	Trebeurden	65
Port Pican	51	Treboul	79
Port-en-Bessin	38	Treguier	62
Portbail	44	Trehiguier	93
Portsall	72	Trentemoult	100
Pourville	30	Trevineuc	105
Primelin	80	Trez Bellec Plage	78
Quiberville	31	Trouville	34
Quineville	40	Ty Anquer	78
Raguenes Plage	83	Vannes	90
Rance Barrage	54	Vers-sur-Mer	38
Regneville-sur-Mer	45	Veules-les-Roses	31
Reville	40	Vierville-sur-Mer	39
Riantec	86	Vilaine River	105
Roscoff	68	Ville Berneuf	57
Rostegoff	78	Wimereux	19
Sangatte	17	Wissant	18
Sangatte South	18	Yport	33
Saumur	108	Zuydcoote	15